Contents

Foreword

THIS series of articles on Steamers of the Clyde, now gathered together and published in book form, first appeared in *Scottish Field* magazine. Originally intended to run for twelve months, the interest which they, and the accompanying paintings, aroused—an interest literally world-wide—extended the series to nearly two years.

The ships selected cover a period of eighty years, from the graceful *Columba* of 1878 to the more utilitarian *Glen Sannox* of 1957. In any selection there must be omissions, but the selection has been made as representative as possible within the limits imposed.

The author, Mr. George Stromier, is an acknowledged authority on the ships of the Clyde and was a co-founder in 1932 of the Clyde River Steamer Club, while Mr. Nicholson is a marine artist of recognised repute. Together they have recorded some of the vessels which formed part of the finest fleet of pleasure steamers in the world.

R.M.S. *Columba*

BY 1877, Mr. David MacBrayne, who had been junior partner in the shipping firm of David Hutcheson and Company, had become virtually the controller; two years later it bore his name.

From the extreme north of the West Highland seaboard down to Loch Fyne Hutcheson boats held the monopoly, so it was something of a shock in that year to find a new enterprise, the Glasgow and Inveraray Steamboat Company, placing a magnificent new vessel called the *Lord of the Isles* on the Inveraray station. Not only were they invading taboo territory but their steamer outclassed every other boat on the Firth—and that included Hutcheson's pride and joy, the *Iona*.

One year in the role of second fiddle was more than enough for Mr. MacBrayne, who thereupon placed an order with J. and G. Thomson of Clydebank for a ship which would eclipse this latest "swan of the Clyde". The outcome was the *Columba*.

Majestic was the only description suitable for her. She was Mr. MacBrayne's showpiece and attained a prestige never before or since reached by any of the river craft. Her fame was worldwide and in the latter months of the Victorian and Edwardian summers the cream of society would board her as a stepping stone on the Royal Route to their shoots and lodges in the Highlands.

Columba's hull, with its curved bow in the pattern of her older "sister" *Iona,* was beautifully modelled and her great oscillating engines ran with great smoothness, driving her through the seas with a placid motion. Her speed placed her among the fleetest of the Clyde greyhounds and her length of over 300 feet has not been equalled in the Clyde passenger fleet. Among her additional appointments were a post office and a barber's shop and in the former department the mail was stamped, sorted and delivered at the various calling points at a rate of over 100,000 letters a month.

Such then was the magnificent vessel which took up the Tarbert and Ardrishaig sailing in 1878 and maintained it for 58 summers with scarce a break in routine.

Columba's voyaging was confined to the holiday months and it was rare for her season to extend into even the first week of October. By that time she was snugly tucked away in Bowling Harbour (Greenock in her latter years) and did not emerge until the following May had run its course. During the Clyde coasting seasons disturbed by the 1914-18 war *Columba* remained in home waters, but did her sailing out of Wemyss Bay, the Cloch-Dunoon boom having curtailed her normal route. She returned to her Glasgow berth when peace was restored.

To the dismay of her countless admirers she appeared for the 1929 season with her glossy black hull painted grey. So great was the outcry against this affront that within the month she was back to her accustomed garb.

At the close of the 1935 summer she retired with the *Iona* to Greenock Harbour for the last time. When they emerged it was but to make the short trip, under tow, to the shipbreaker's yard at Dalmuir.

R.M.S. "COLUMBA"   J. NICHOLSON.

P.S. Ivanhoe

PASSENGERS who imbibed well rather than wisely became something of a problem on the Clyde river steamers in the 19th century, so much so that in the 1870's a consortium of businessmen decided to run a vessel on strictly teetotal lines. They formed the Frith of Clyde Steam Packet Company and on February 25, 1880, a 225-foot long paddle steamer was launched at the yard of D. and W. Henderson. She was given the name *Ivanhoe* and although she made her headquarters at Helensburgh she was not connected with the North British fleet then based there. After the launch the guests were entertained by the builders in the model-room at Meadowside, when a rather incongruous note was struck by the speeches being toasted in wine!

The *Ivanhoe* was a twin funnel saloon steamer, typical of the period, with narrow alleyways running down the outside of the main and fore saloons. The normal refreshment bars, however, were conspicuous by their absence. On May 3 she underwent her trials and at the beginning of June went into service. On her opening cruise she encountered both the *Glen Rosa* and the *Sheila* on the route to Arran when, sad to relate, the new ship came off worst.

Her daily run was by way of Greenock Custom House Quay, Princes Pier, Kirn, Dunoon, Wemyss Bay, Rothesay, Tighnabruaich, Corrie and Brodick to Lamlash. On Mondays, Wednesdays, and Fridays she extended her voyage to King's Cross and Whiting Bay. During her first season a special extra run was made on Saturdays either to Campbeltown, round Arran or round Ailsa Craig. Later on Pladda was the objective of the extra sail and still later gave way to an evening cruise, a form of excursion which this steamer inaugurated and popularised.

Another new steamer, the *Scotia*, had to deputise for the *Ivanhoe* in the first week of her service as the *Ivanhoe* broke down after leaving Wemyss Bay and had to be towed into Rothesay by the steam yacht *Matador*. Her first two seasons, however, were so successful that in September, 1881, the local press carried a report that four Clyde yards had been asked to estimate for building three more steamers to expand the Firth of Clyde Company's business.

Under the command of Captain James Williamson, who was also part owner, the *Ivanhoe* continued to prosper (although she did not get any additional fleet units to assist her). Captain Williamson left her at the close of the decade to become Marine Superintendent of the new Caledonian Steam Packet Company.

In the spring of 1894 the *Ivanhoe* went south for the opening of the Manchester Ship Canal but was back in her native waters for the start of the summer season. Three years later she was bought outright by the C.S.P. Company—although to all intents and purposes she had been plying under their supervision for some time—and bars were installed.

Her new owners placed her on ordinary coast connections from the railway termini and she was no longer regarded as a cruise boat. The year 1911 found her again changing hands, this time on the Broomielaw run, for a firm known as the Firth of Clyde Steam Packet Company. They changed her yellow funnels to white and later added narrow black tops. By 1914 she was in the hands of Turbine Steamers Limited, who lengthened the black funnel tops to the conventional depth. She was running frequently to Lochgoilhead at this time but when the war curtailed the sailings she was chartered to the Caledonian company and once again became a railway boat. At first she ran from Rothesay to Wemyss Bay but later was engaged solely above the Dunoon-Cloch boom on the Gourock, Kirn, Dunoon station.

In 1920 the *Ivanhoe* was handed back to Turbine Steamers but lay in harbour at Greenock until she made the sad passage to the breaker's yard at Dumbarton.

P.S. 'IVANHOE'

J. NICHOLSON

P.S. Grenadier

THE MacBrayne fleet down the years has included some really handsome vessels, but there was surely no finer looking craft to carry the famous red and black funnel than the *Grenadier*, launched in March, 1885, from the Clydebank yard of J. and G. Thomson.

This statement must be qualified to exclude the first 16 years of *Grenadier's* existence. Originally she possessed two rather spindly looking funnels which detracted from the balanced beauty of her hull design, but after she was reboiled in 1902, the sight of her graceful form gliding over the Firth of Clyde or West Highland waters was sufficient to gladden the heart of any artist.

The *Grenadier*, 222 feet in length, had full-width saloons both fore and aft, brightened by the insertion of large observation windows. Under her fiddle bow and bowsprit she carried the carved figure of a grenadier. A pair of oscillating engines gave her a speed of a little over 16 knots.

Although *Grenadier* put in many weeks of service in her 42 years, she was strictly speaking hardly a Clyde pleasure steamer. Much of her time was spent outwith the Clyde estuary with Oban as her base and it was only in the off season that she put in an appearance on MacBrayne's Ardrishaig run.

Having completed her trial trip through the Kyles of Bute to Glen Sannox, Arran and back to Princes Pier, *Grenadier's* first service was to Loch Fyne until the *Columba* relieved her early in June, 1885. Then she made her way round the Mull of Kintyre to Crinan and ran from there to Oban and Fort William. At the height of the season she was transferred to the Oban, Loch Scavaig, Loch Coruisk, Portree and Gairloch run. Later she took over the Staffa and Iona cruise and was identified with this route almost continuously throughout her career.

There was a break in continuity after reboiling in the winter of 1902/3. The ensuing summer saw her on the Clyde with her headquarters at Rothesay, where she left each morning at 8.15 for the Broomielaw, retracing her path each afternoon at 1.30. On Saturdays she extended her route to Tighnabruaich and circled the Island of Bute.

As one would expect of a vessel designed for open water work, *Grenadier* proved a useful unit in the Royal Navy's minesweeping service during the 1914-18 war. Her naval service was without incident and she returned to Irvine in March, 1919, for reconditioning and was soon back on her summer service to Iona.

Grenadier's peace-time activities were in contrast to her carefree naval career. In January, 1902, she damaged her stern in a collision with a dock wall. Five years later her figurehead had to be replaced after she had collided with another vessel, and in November of the same year she ran aground and was holed off Gourock during a dense fog on the Firth.

Further trouble was avoided until January, 1925, when, though in fine fettle after overhaul (she was clipping 25 minutes off her normal time between Rothesay and Ardrishaig), she broke a shaft. She was back on duty, however, within a fortnight. But disaster fell on the night of September 6, 1927, while she lay at the North Pier, Oban. Fire broke out and spread so rapidly that three of her crew failed to escape. One of the victims was her master, Captain Archibald McArthur.

After being made seaworthy and the paddlewheels removed, *Grenadier* was towed to Greenock, but a fuller inspection confirmed that the damage was beyond practical repair. The hull was towed to Ardrossan for dismantling and thus passed from active service the bonniest paddleboat to fly the MacBrayne colours.

P.S. 'GRENADIER'

J. NICHOLSON.

S.S. *Davaar*

To replace a paddle steamer called *Gael*, which had gone south to join the Great Western Railway fleet, the Campbeltown and Glasgow Steam Packet Joint Stock Company had the *Davaar* built in 1885 by the London and Glasgow Shipbuilding Yard at Govan.

The Campbeltown company had been in the shipping business since 1826. All their vessels had been paddle driven until 1869, when the *Kintyre* started the vogue of screw propulsion and yacht-like hull design, even down to the bowsprit. *Kinloch* followed the same pattern 10 years later and *Davaar* carried on the tradition, which was to end with her demise.

Davaar possessed only moderate speed but made up for this deficiency by her seaworthiness which was a necessity for her all-the-year-round duties. The Kilbrannan Sound could be a dirty stretch of water in the winter months.

As built, *Davaar* had two rather thin funnels set close together, but when reboiled in 1903 a single funnel of greater diameter was fitted, a change which enhanced her appearance. At this time, too, the main saloon aft, which had alleyways down each side, was widened to the full breadth of the ship. The promenade deck above the saloon was extended to the stern, but the side plating terminated with the saloon, leaving approximately some 15 feet at the rear open to the elements.

With *Kintyre* and *Kinloch* using the Glasgow terminal, *Davaar* maintained a daily service to Campbeltown from Custom House Quay, Greenock, with calls at Princes Pier, Gourock, Lochranza, Pirnmill, Carradale and Saddell until 1907 when *Kintyre* was lost off Skelmorlie. *Davaar* then went up river to join *Kinloch*.

Twelve years earlier *Davaar* herself had all but broken up the partnership of the " three graceful sisters." Since the earliest days the townsfolk of Campbeltown had enjoyed a bi-annual excursion to Belfast and on June 7, 1895, *Davaar* was on this run. On entering Belfast Lough she ran into dense fog and grounded on a rocky stretch of the coastline known as Brigg's Reef. All the passengers were taken ashore safely but when the tide dropped *Davaar's* bows were left rearing high in the air and she was in danger of breaking her back. But she proved a stout craft and was successfully refloated after two days of anxiety and suspense. One of the rescue tugs sent to her assistance was not so fortunate, running over a submerged wreck and sinking.

Davaar returned to her route in less than a week and sailed for the rest of her career as consort to *Kinloch* and later to *Dalriada*.

During the 1914-18 war she continued on the Campbeltown service, running for a short period in 1915 from Ardrossan as base and latterly from Wemyss Bay because of the submarine defence boom at Dunoon.

In 1937 a change in ownership in the Clyde and Campbeltown Company saw the familiar black funnel with broad red band give place to one of red with black top.

In the Second World War, with the threat of invasion in 1940, *Davaar* sailed south for Newhaven, where she was to be sunk as a blockship at the harbour entrance. Fortunately this did not become necessary, but she never again raised steam. When the danger had passed she was beached on the Sussex coast and scrapped in 1943.

S.S. DAVAAR

J. NICHOLSON.

P.S. Madge Wildfire

ALTHOUGH she started her career as *Madge Wildfire* and carried this title for the first 27 years of her life, this little paddle steamer is probably better remembered as the *Isle of Skye*.

The "Madge" entered the ranks of the Clyde river steamer fleet in 1886 as one of Captain Campbell's Holy Loch boats. She was a product of McKnight's yard in Ayr. At this time the Campbells had two vessels on the route, the *Meg Merrilies* and the *Waverley*, but the latter was too large and too fast for this service and was transferred to the Ayr route when the *Madge Wildfire* made her appearance.

Ideally suited for the daily run to Kilmun from the Broomielaw, doing a steady 16 knots in the process, there was nothing particularly outstanding about the "Madge". She had only one saloon, a plainly furnished affair which extended from midships to near the stern.

After only three seasons with her original owners she changed hands. The Caledonian Steam Packet company had just come into being and for a start they purchased the goodwill, stock and business of the Campbell concern. *Madge Wildfire* then changed her all-white funnel for the all-yellow one of the latest Clyde shipowners. She was kept on her usual route for a number of years and later served the Holy Loch from Gourock. Her new masters evidently found her a more than useful boat as they kept her for the best part of a quarter of a century, during which period she deputised on occasion on the Millport or Rothesay runs. They also fitted her with a small foresaloon and, in 1903, transferred the bridge forward of the funnel and redesigned her paddleboxes from the fan shaped style to the horizontal slotted pattern.

In 1911 she again changed hands. A Captain Cameron of Dumbarton decided to go in for steamboat owning and his first acquisition was *Madge Wildfire*. In his service she made an assortment of cruises to the coastal resorts. It was apparently a paying proposition, for in the next year she was joined by another unit, the erstwhile North British steamer *Lady Rowena*. *Madge Wildfire's* sojourn with Cameron was of only two years' duration yet she managed to change the colour of her funnel twice. In her first year she had merely added a black top to her yellow "lum", but the next season the

yellow was replaced by red. In this condition the hull was repainted in an unusual hue for the Clyde fleet—bottle green.

The 1913 change was to Buchanan. This fleet was short of a vessel after the departure of the *Isle of Bute* for service in Morecambe Bay, so *Madge Wildfire* was bought in as a replacement and renamed *Isle of Skye*, with her funnel in the Buchanan colours of black with white band. She made her first run under the Buchanan flag on the 10.30 a.m. service from the Broomielaw to Dunoon, Rothesay and the Kyles of Bute. Thereafter she was placed on the 11 o'clock run.

In the first two years of the war she was still running from the Broomielaw, often to Millport before the anti-submarine boom was laid and then into the Gareloch, but by 1916 her name had disappeared from the Clyde fleet. The Admiralty had called her up as a fleet auxiliary and she saw service as a tender in the Cromarty Firth and as a minesweeper in the Pentland Firth.

After three years of strenuous naval work the little paddlesteamer came back to a much changed Clyde scene in March, 1919. The Williamson and Buchanan interests had merged to form a new company and the *Isle of Skye* was the first vessel to sail for them.

Once again her funnel colouring had undergone a change. The Navy had painted her grey all over and her 1919 ensemble was white and black topped funnel, black hull and paddleboxes. Mostly she was on the Rothesay service with spells on the Millport run.

Early in 1927 Williamson-Buchanan sold her to the Grangemouth and Forth Towing Company Limited. Based at Leith and with her name changed to *Fair Maid* she made daily trips from Leith West Pier to Aberdour, Kirkcaldy and under the Forth Bridge to Kincardine and Alloa. The funnel, of course, was again repainted; this time to black top and buff base.

When war came again in 1939 the *Fair Maid* was beyond active service but, garbed once again in grey, she was transformed into a decontamination vessel. The end of hostilities also saw the end of the little ship; she was broken up at Troon.

In one respect *Fair Maid*, ex *Isle of Skye*, ex *Madge Wildfire* was surely unique among Clyde steamers; she sported no fewer than nine successive colour schemes on her well proportioned funnel.

P.S. 'MADGE WILDFIRE'

J. NICHOLSON.

P.S. Lucy Ashton

THE *Dandie Dinmont,* one of the original ships of the North British when they began their Clyde service in 1866, was, after 22 years, deemed obsolete. To replace her, an order was given to Thomas Seath and Company of Rutherglen, and in May, 1888, the *Lucy Ashton* successfully negotiated the weir, went down river for completion and joined the other Sir Walter Scott "characters" *Jeanie Deans, Guy Mannering, Diana Vernon* and the little *Gareloch* to give her services to Dunoon, the Holy Loch and occasional trips to Rothesay.

There was nothing outstanding in either the design or machinery of the new ship, although she certainly possessed a beautifully modelled hull. She had a comfortable but not lavish saloon aft, a miniature and rather austere one forward, a haystack boiler and a single diagonal engine capable of driving her at something under 17 knots. All in all a handy little craft but definitely playing second fiddle to the two greyhounds already established in the fleet.

Later additions at Craigendoran relegated her to the Gareloch run but if this was a more sheltered route that escaped the winter gales of the open Firth there were other hazards just as threatening. The Gareloch was seldom free of laid up liners and while these could be easily avoided during the hours of sunshine they were a deadly menace in fog or bad weather.

Thus it was in December, 1910, during a severe snowstorm, that the Allan liner *Siberian* dragged her anchor and lay full in the track usually traversed by the *Lucy Ashton.* The little Craigendoran paddleboat ran full tilt into the merchantman and had her bows stove in. Although badly crippled she got back to headquarters. Had she not been a worthy example of Clyde shipbuilding art a worse fate might have befallen her.

For close on 40 years the *Lucy Ashton* did the selfsame run plus the ferry service over to Princes Pier. She escaped the call to the colours in both world wars and remained at home, a useful prop in the depleted Clyde passenger steamer ranks.

The Second World War saw her embark on the most strenuous period of her career. Although in her fifties, she was the sole unit of the Craigendoran fleet and carried on year after year with scarcely a pause in service. Necessary overhauls were usually performed on Sundays as she lay at her base.

Before the lifting of the anti-submarine boom her run did not extend beyond Dunoon, but when this was raised in 1945 she re-opened the Craigendoran-Rothesay sailings and kept up this duty until the return of the *Talisman* and *Jeanie Deans* from war service.

With the nationalisation of the railways in 1948 the *Lucy Ashton* lost the funnel colouring of red, white and black with which the Craigendoran boats were associated . . . albeit during the war years her "lum" had been painted grey . . . and donned the less distinguished livery of buff and black.

Towards the close of her career the old ship had risen in eminence from the position of one of the lesser lights of a once mighty fleet. She had won for herself an affection from war-weary Clydeside that surpassed that of any other vessel previously connected with the Clyde passenger trade. The Clyde River Steamer Club honoured her diamond jubilee with a special charter, when for a brief afternoon she revisited many of her old haunts.

But in 1949 the writing was on the wall and she was towed to Faslane for breaking up. Souvenir hunters abounded and her siren was purchased by a Glasgow firm and given to a business in Santiago, Chile, where its high pitched tone still calls the workers to duty.

The Lucy's hull was retrieved from the breaker's yard and used for a brief spell by the British Shipbuilders Research Association in experimental tests connected with jet propulsion.

With the departure of the *Lucy Ashton,* the Clyde passenger service severed its last link with the Victorian era.

P.S. "LUCY ASHTON" (1888-1949)   J. NICHOLSON. 1953.

P.S. Duchess of Hamilton

THE year after their debut on the Firth of Clyde the Caledonian Steam Packet Company added three new ships to their fleet, one of which was a very notable vessel, the *Duchess of Hamilton*.

Built and engined by Denny at Dumbarton and launched in April, 1890, she was a lengthy boat of 250 feet. Her spaciousness was accentuated by the then novel design of having the promenade deck extended right forward to the bow and very nearly to the stern. The main saloon aft, furnished in the most luxurious Victorian style, was the full breadth of the vessel. Strangely enough, although the C.S.P.'s other new ships had foresaloons of similar width, the *Duchess of Hamilton* had alleyways running down each side.

To Captain James Williamson, then Marine Superintendent of the Caley, she was the finest river steamer ever to grace the waters of the Clyde and he continued to laud her praises long after the arrival of newer tonnage. Despite his acclaim the "Duchess" was not as graceful as some of her sister "Duchesses," nor could she be included in the greyhound class for long. There was a noticeable absence of lift and sheer forward and on her vast expanse of deck the funnel and bridge were placed too close together to give a pleasing outline. But for all that she was a fine vessel. Designed as an 18-knotter she is recorded as having touched 18·1 knots on trial and is said to have held the *Columba* in a trial of speed in her first year—no mean feat. She lost pace, however, fairly early in her career.

In the year of her launch the Caledonian Railway had opened their route to Ardrossan in opposition to the Glasgow and South Western and the *Duchess of Hamilton* was intended to cater for the Arran trade. The Sou' West connection on this sea link was the Buchanan steamer *Scotia* and when the Caledonian representative appeared on

the scene she had little difficulty in vanquishing her old-fashioned opponent. In two brief years, however, the opposition had secured the nucleus of a fleet of their own planning and, with the advent of the *Neptune* and that quite remarkable craft the *Glen Sannox*, it was the turn of the yellow funnel steamer to play second fiddle.

Nevertheless the *Duchess of Hamilton* remained a firm favourite on the Arran route and when she was transferred up river to Gourock in 1906 to make way for the *Duchess of Argyll*, she carried her popularity with her. Here she was employed mostly on excursion work—Round the Lochs, Round Arran and Ailsa Craig or Ayr and Ailsa Craig—and was also a ready choice as club steamer at many of the Clyde regattas. In June, 1909, the Caley introduced the first Sunday rail connection to the coast and the "Duchess" performed this run. By 1911 she had changed her week-day schedule and was sailing daily to Arrochar.

The "Duchess" had one or two mishaps while serving on the Firth but they were all of a minor character. She was also in the news as a rescue ship, like the time in 1899 when she found the *Jupiter* out of action with a stiff north-westerly gale blowing. The *Duchess of Hamilton* was on her last run of the day from Ardrossan when she encountered the *Jupiter* one and a half miles off the Arran coast. She stood by until tugs were summoned, then took off her rival's passengers and landed them on the mainland.

In the first World War she was commandeered as a naval auxiliary and, after some time on trooping duties, was fitted out for minesweeping. In this capacity, while in the company of the Thames pleasure steamer *Yarmouth Belle*, she was sunk on November 29, 1915, unfortunately with the loss of some of her crew, one of whom had served on her in peacetime on the Firth of Clyde.

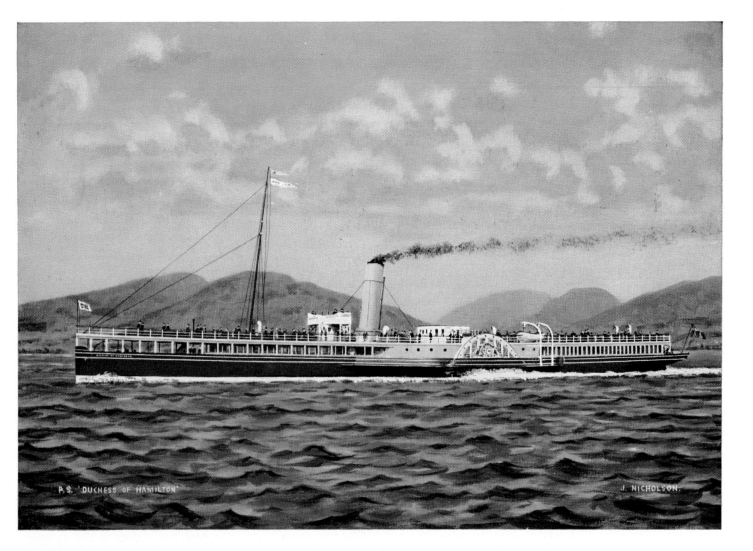

P.S. 'DUCHESS OF HAMILTON'   J. NICHOLSON.

P.S. *Lord of the Isles*

AN Inveraray service via Dunoon, Rothesay and the Kyles of Bute was inaugurated in 1877 when a new company, the Glasgow and Inveraray Steamboat Company, placed a steamer which they named *Lord of the Isles* on this route. A highly successful vessel, she maintained this run for 13 summers before being bought by a London concern for service on the Thames.

To replace her for the 1891 season, the same builders, Messrs. D. and W. Henderson, Partick, were given the contract to construct a second and more up to date version, and so a second paddleboat bearing the title *Lord of the Isles* made her appearance on the Firth.

She was another extremely fine craft and a delight to the eye. Her widely spaced funnels of multicoloured design, backed by burnished copper steam pipes, helped to enhance her smart appearance. Unlike her predecessor, the saloons were built to the full width of the hull. Originally the foresaloon terminated just abaft the mast, but in 1895 the promenade deck was extended to the bow, giving her greatly increased carrying capacity. With a good turn of speed, the " Lord " maintained the high standard which her forerunner had established.

For the first dozen years of her existence she plied the Inveraray trade with great success, monarch of all she surveyed in Loch Fyne, but when the turbine *King Edward* appeared on the scene her monopoly ceased. Gradually the old paddle steamer's complements began to dwindle and in 1912 Turbine Steamers Limited bought her and she was given a new route to travel. Starting at the Broomielaw daily at 10.30 she traversed the same course as far as Tighnabruaich, but then headed south to circumvent the Island of Bute before turning homeward.

The *Lord of the Isles* was not requisitioned when war came in 1914 but sailed on from Glasgow to Lochgoilhead, as the anti-submarine defence boom barred her way southward beyond Dunoon. When the river was temporarily closed to cruising traffic she made her headquarters at Princes Pier.

After the armistice she resumed the " round Bute " run until the final year of her existence, 1928.

Having suffered a double blow in 1927 through the loss of both the *Chevalier* and *Grenadier*, MacBrayne's fleet was under strength, so the *Lord of the Isles* flew the famous West Highland pennant in her last year in service, on the Lochgoil and Arrochar route. At the end of the season she was condemned and on October 24 was towed from Bowling Harbour to Port Glasgow for breaking up.

In a lifespan of 39 years, entirely free from mishap, she was served by only three captains, Donald Downie, Archie McAllister and Allan McDougall. The first mentioned had stepped from the bridge of the first " Lord " to his new command.

With her departure the Clyde not only lost a famous steamer, but another distinctive funnel colouring passed from the scene.

P.S. "LORD OF THE ISLES"   J. NICHOLSON.

P.S. Glen Rosa

IF for no other reason the *Glen Rosa* may be remembered as the last surviving member of the great Glasgow and South Western fleet. This company, which was later than the Caledonian and the North British in acquiring vessels to maintain its Clyde coast service, began operations with second-hand ships in 1891. The following year three new vessels were built and in 1893 two more were ordered, of which the *Glen Rosa* was to be one. Shortly after construction began at Clydebank the Belfast and County Down Railway took over one of the ships, naming her *Slieve Donard.* The two vessels were almost identical, but one had a more graceful sheer forward and aft. The Scottish railway claimed this boat and she took the name *Minerva.* A third craft, identical to the Irish vessel, was then laid down and she became *Glen Rosa*.

Built to sturdy specifications, *Glen Rosa* and her near twin were intended for off season work on the Firth and to help out where required during the summer months. The promenade deck was not carried far beyond the mast, but the cutaway bow was covered over at bulwark level and railed off. The front end of the foresaloon was extensively strengthened and altogether a more formidable pair of winter boats could not be found anywhere. In the engine room the powerful little pair of diagonals were smaller editions of the heavy machinery characteristic of the Princes Pier boats and produced a good turn of speed. Towards the close of her career *Glen Rosa* had lost pace to a marked degree and those who were unfamiliar with her early success as a pacemaker were apt to hold her to ridicule.

She opened her career with a variety of cruises and when the summer had gone took up the winter run to Arran from Ardrossan.

No Clyde steamer was better suited for this arduous task. *Glen Rosa* also appeared for a spell on the Loch Long route and took part in tendering work from Princes Pier.

During the First World War she acted as minesweeper, chiefly in the Belfast Lough and Irish Sea, when she bore the title H.M.S. *Glencross.* She was one of a group with the *Kenilworth, Talisman, Caledonia, Marchioness of Bute, Marchioness of Breadalbane* and *Isle of Arran.* When the flotilla moved south to operate in the English Channel *Glen Rosa* dropped out at Swansea to join another group.

On her return to the Clyde her summer season running was almost entirely devoted to the Millport and Kilchattan Bay route, at first from Fairlie and later from Wemyss Bay when she came under L.M.S. control.

Throughout her entire career only once do I know of her being in trouble. That was in March, 1930, when on the evening run from Ardrossan to Arran. A bracket in her port paddle snapped when on passage between Brodick and Lamlash. She was only a quarter of a mile offshore in Corriegills Bay and, as the sea was calm, she anchored. After her passengers had been landed by ship's boat the Clyde Shipping Company's tug *Flying Swallow* towed her to Greenock.

Glen Rosa continued to serve the Cumbrae until the final year of her existence when, as in her initial season, she was engaged in an assortment of cruises from the Clyde resorts.

Just before the declaration of war in 1939 she was taken to Arnott Young's at Dalmuir and broken up.

P.S. "GLEN ROSA"

J. NICHOLSON.

P.S. Culzean Castle

THE season of 1895 found an "un-kent face" among the Clyde pleasure fleet, the paddle steamer *Culzean Castle*. Built at Southampton in 1891, she had been the property of the Bournemouth, Poole and Swanage Steam Packet Company, when she was known as *Windsor Castle*. A Scottish concern, the Glasgow, Ayrshire and Campbeltown Steamboat Company, judging her to be ideal for their service to Kintyre, purchased her and brought her north.

The *Culzean Castle* was a big, beamy boat of 254 feet and was reputed to have touched 19 knots on her trials. She had a large single elliptical buff and black-topped funnel, two masts and saloons fore and aft, the former stretching just short of the foremast. Her bow was yacht-like in design but, strange to say, for a time she carried no bowsprit. In the forepeak there was an ample forecastle raised to the level of the promenade deck. Two other features of her design were novel on the Clyde. The saloons were lit by rounded ports instead of by conventional windows and in the engine room the machinery was a triple crank drive.

After a hurried overhaul she was put into service on the first day of June, 1895, under the command of Captain Alexander Gillies, late of Buchanan's steamer *Eagle*. Her run was from Princes Pier to Campbeltown, via Dunoon, Fairlie, Keppel, Lochranza, Pirnmill and Machrie Bay.

During her first season she suffered from machinery trouble; on one occasion an engine seizure on her way back from Campbeltown so delayed her that she berthed at Keppel in the region of 1 a.m. and still had to thread her way to her upper Firth base. Worst of all she suffered a further engine failure during Glasgow Fair and the *Glenmore* had to be hurriedly chartered from John Williamson to deputise for her. On yet another occasion her electricity system failed and she returned to her base with emergency oil lighting illuminating her way.

During the following close season she had a substantial overhaul. The saloons were refurnished, new steam steering was fitted, the main mast was removed and the welldeck covered over, so that the promenade deck formed one continuous line with the level of the forecastle. The deck below the new extension, however, was not plated in. A bowsprit was added, and with her funnel changed to red she was ready for a fresh start. Unfortunately her performance was not improved and eventually, with the threat of the turbine era in the air, Williamson's *Strathmore* took over the Campbeltown route.

Under the flag of Clyde Excursion Steamers Ltd. she assumed her third name, *Carrick Castle*, and was based at Glasgow, giving an assortment of cruises from the Broomielaw. She was also open for charter work and in August, 1899, took part in an unusual excursion from Campbeltown to the Isle of Man. The *Carrick Castle* conveyed the trippers on the first leg of their journey from Campbeltown to Stranraer, where they entrained for Garlieston, sailing the rest of the way to Douglas in the Isle of Man Steam Packet's boat *Prince of Wales*.

The following year proved to be *Carrick Castle's* last on the Clyde. M. T. Clark was now managing her and she was engaged mostly in making runs to the Kyles of Bute. This final season was indeed a short one, only from the Queen's Birthday Holiday until early August. Then she proceeded to Govan Dry Dock for strengthening in order to face the winds and waves beyond the Clyde. Her new masters were the Russian-owned Chinese Eastern Railway and her new headquarters were at Port Arthur under yet another new title, *Nagadan*.

When the Russo-Japanese war broke out in 1904 she was used as a fleet auxiliary. The Japanese troops advanced with such rapidity that they thwarted an attempt to blow up the *Nagadan* and she was captured intact. After the war she ran under the Japanese flag, first as the *Nagara Maru* and later as the *Tenri Maru*. In November, 1931, she went ashore at Matsu Shima, Japan. This may well have been the swansong of a Clyde passenger steamer which somehow never quite made the grade.

P.S. "CULZEAN CASTLE"

J. NICHOLSON.

P.S. Juno

THE last addition to the Glasgow and South Western fleet before the turn of the century was the *Juno* from the Clydebank Ship-building and Engineering Company. Some mystery surrounds her introduction into the railway ranks. In the eighteen nineties new vessels destined for the Firth received a wheen of publicity right from the laying down of the keel, yet *Juno* made her debut almost unheralded. Not until the last days of June, 1898, did a small paragraph appear in the Press announcing that the new paddle steamer completing at Clydebank was named *Juno* and would run for the G. & S.W. Rumour has it that she was originally intended for the South Coast and came to the Clyde services, in a manner of speaking, secondhand.

Juno was a big vessel by Clyde standards, with a girth that fitted her for work in any weather. Her powerful engines could drive her at over 19 knots, as she proved on her trials over the Skelmorlie mile on July 5, 1898.

Her first call was at Rothesay three days later with a party of Greenock excursionists bound for Ayr and thenceforth she made Ayr her base. This gave her all too few opportunities to display her prowess as a racer unless she encountered a rival on some of her cruises up Firth to the Gareloch, Loch Long, Rothesay or the Kyles of Bute. Much of her sailing was done towards Arran and she made weekly trips to Stranraer, where she remained overnight while her passengers returned by rail.

Juno was really a summer " butterfly boat " although she occasionally filled in in spring and autumn (while some of her colleagues were overhauling) by running from Princes Pier.

Because of her weatherly qualities *Juno* was the first Clyde enlistment to the white ensign when war was declared in 1914. She served from February, 1915, until April, 1919, under the rather misleading title of H.M.S. *Junior*.

Juno was also one of the first Clyde passenger boats to be demobbed and was a useful asset to the scanty fleet operating in the initial post-war summer when she maintained the Rothesay and Kyles of Bute service for the G. & S.W. Her first run was made on June 28 after a speedy reconditioning at Barclay Curle's yard. Soon she was back to her old haunt of Ayr, but no longer cruised to Stranraer as in pre-war days.

Her proud record of freedom from mishap ended in July, 1920, when she broke two brackets in her paddlewheel a mile south of Ailsa Craig. With the assistance of the tug at Ayr she was taken back to port and later up Firth.

In 1923 she came under L.M.S. control and it was not long before her graceful grey hull had been changed to black and the red base of her tall, slightly elliptical funnel turned to buff.

Most of the South Western boats were rather notorious for their coal consumption and as such were none too popular with their new London managers. *Glen Sannox* had already been withdrawn from service when, in 1931, the economy axe terminated the career of the big, beamy, beautiful *Juno*. She made her last run on September 12 and the following February was sent to Alloa for breaking up.

P.S. JUNO   J. NICHOLSON.

T.S. King Edward

THE service to Campbeltown had been for many years in the hands of the local concern, the Campbeltown and Glasgow Steam Packet Joint Stock Company, when in the nineties a boat called the *Herald* made daily runs from Fairlie; later another paddleboat, the *Culzean Castle* appeared on the same route. There had also been odd day excursions to the Kintyre capital by a host of other Clyde pleasure steamers but towards the close of the century the Williamsons decided to compete for this traffic. Their paddle steamer *Strathmore* was put on the run, but she was only a *pro tem* stand-in for a revolutionary new vessel which was shortly to make her debut . . . a turbine propelled craft. There had been screw vessels before in the Clyde fleet, but they had all been driven by reciprocating engines.

Sir Charles Parsons had so successfully demonstrated the merits of his invention with his experimental ship *Turbinia* that the Admiralty ordered two new destroyers to be turbine powered, but when the *King Edward* appeared on the Clyde she was the first commercial turbine-driven ship in the world.

In 1901 Denny of Dumbarton launched the new Williamson boat. Her attractive appearance and her speed of more than 20 knots, coupled with the smoothness of her running, made her an instant success. Below decks she was fitted out in the conventional manner of the paddle steamer of her day, although the public missed the thrilling sight of whirling cranks when " visiting the engines."

So effective was she on service that the following year another and larger turbine, *Queen Alexandra,* appeared on the scene and a new route had to be worked out for the pioneer. By 1902 she was sailing via Dunoon, Fairlie and Rothesay to Tarbert and Ardrishaig round the Garroch Head. Later her run was extended to Inveraray. Here she clashed with the well established *Lord of the Isles*, but eventually forced the old paddleboat off the route.

After successful work as a troopship in the English Channel in the First World War she was kitted out as a hospital ship for a run to Archangel. Her return voyage from Russia was a perilous one owing to the extreme stress of weather and she docked at Aberdeen many days overdue.

Peacetime found her back on the Campbeltown run, from which she deviated rarely until, with the advent of the *King George V* in 1926, she came up river to join the Williamson-Buchanan " all the way " fleet.

King Edward's adventures did not end with her war-time experiences. In July, 1925, she was run into by the *Duchess of Argyll* off Largs and escaped possible foundering by the stoutness of the belting round her hull.

Although remaining in home waters throughout the period of the Second World War she had another alarming experience when a collision with the *Lairdsburn* resulted in a great hole being torn in her bow. Later, in the late forties, she was an innocent but unfortunate bystander when a tow rope between a tug and a large cargo vessel was accidentally swept across her foredeck, snapping off her mast.

By this time she was a unit of the nationalised Clyde fleet and was frequently pressed into service for railway connections at the coast termini.

Shortly after celebrating her golden jubilee, the *King Edward* was withdrawn from service and taken to Troon for breaking up.

The estuary lost a notable vessel with the passing of this old favourite. In an era which has witnessed the rise and dominance of the diesel engine with its attendant noise and vibration, her tranquillity of motion would have been all the more pronounced, for despite her age *King Edward's* machinery appeared to be running as smoothly as the day she pioneered turbine propulsion on the Clyde.

T.S. "KING EDWARD"

J. NICHOLSON.

P.S. Duchess of Fife

TO augment their fleet the Caledonian Steam Packet Company in 1902 had the paddle steamer *Duchess of Montrose* built for them by John Brown's. She was a pretty little ship, of a handy pattern that made her ideal for all-the-year-round work, but of only moderate pace. The following year the C.S.P. Company required a duplicate order, so pleased had they been with their latest acquisition. Whether through pressure of other business at Clydebank, I know not, but the contract finally went to Fairfield.

This was actually the first Clyde passenger steamer constructed in the Govan yard and so successful were the builders that one is tempted to think that the order was long overdue.

Fairfield turned out a really splendid job, very similar to the "Duchess" of the previous year, and even managed to coax an extra knot or two through the finely balanced ratio of hull line and engine power.

The year 1903, then, saw the *Duchess of Fife*, as the new boat was called, sally forth to join the "other titled ladies of Gourock." Originally she possessed a surprising turn of speed that enabled her to compete, often successfully, with higher powered craft and as a winter boat she was the essence of efficiency.

Her life started on the Rothesay section with its attendant afternoon cruise to the Kyles of Bute, but so versatile was the "wee Fife" that she has been known to deputise even for the turbine *Queen Alexandra* on the Campbeltown route.

She saw service in both world wars. In the first she was exclusively used as a minesweeper and was based on Grimsby but in the second her naval duties were more varied. As a unit of the 12th Minesweeping Flotilla she was in company with the other Clyde favourites *Waverley, Marmion* and *Eagle III* and helped to succour the beleagured forces on the Dunkirk beaches. Convoy and ferry duties followed before she was ready to resume her peace-time role.

Her first job on her return was on the Holy Loch run. Unfortunately her engine seized up as she lay at Kilmun on the afternoon schedule and her passengers were returned to Gourock via bus to Dunoon and then by another steamer. Thereafter she became associated with the Wemyss Bay-Largs-Millport and Kilchattan Bay route till the close of her illustrious career in June, 1953. She was broken up at Port Glasgow in the autumn of that year.

Apart from going ashore in dense fog near Kirn in 1936 her career was entirely free from incident, which was a fine record for a vessel which saw Clyde service in and out of season.

The change over in the Clyde fleet to diesel driven Maids and car ferries was the swan song of the little *Duchess of Fife*, a vessel which had rightly earned the designation "the ideal hull model and design for a Clyde passenger steamer."

P.S. DUCHESS OF FIFE

J. NICHOLSON. 1963.

P.S. Marmion

AFTER the North British had launched their most outstanding vessel, the *Waverley*, at the close of the 19th century, seven years were to elapse before there was an addition to the ranks. Then came the *Marmion*, from the same yard, A. and J. Inglis of Pointhouse. She was more or less a smaller and less powerful version of her famous predecessor. Again the foresaloon was carried well forward of the mast, with a short low bow. The only appreciable difference in general outline was the arrangement of the bridge forward of the funnel instead of between the paddleboxes.

With her well raked red, white and black funnel, a lavish application of gilt for adornment and a general neatness of design, she was altogether most pleasing to the eye. Internally, too, *Marmion* was a big advance on anything that had appeared at Craigendoran, in fact her well designed furnishings were never bettered in a Clyde steamer.

March 12, 1906, saw the new boat running her trials on the Gareloch measured mile where she clocked 17.3 knots, not a great speed, but the excessive demands for pace that had prevailed in the nineties no longer held. She then embarked on a cruise up and down Lochs Long and Goil, skirted Dunoon, Innellan and Toward and on to the Kyles of Bute before returning to headquarters.

She replaced *Redgauntlet* on the Arrochar cruise and gave the Holy Loch commuters a morning and evening service. This routine was followed until 1915, when in April she was called for naval duties as a minesweeper. For this service the Admiralty altered her considerably, extending the promenade deck to the bow and plating in the hull.

After a fairly uneventful career under the white ensign she returned to the Clyde for the 1920 season. The structural alterations carried out for war service were retained but they had affected her trim and greatly impaired her handling at piers.

Marmion was on the Arrochar run once more until the reappearance of the *Waverley* in July, when she was transferred to the Rothesay route. At the end of the summer she retired to Bowling Harbour and did not re-emerge until 1926. By then the fleet was sailing under the L.N.E.R. flag, and she replaced the *Dandie Dinmont,* which eventually went to the Hull-New Holland car ferry service. *Marmion* came out to rejoin her colleagues with her foresaloon considerably shortened (it barely reached beyond the bridge) and if she was no longer the " beauty queen " of her youth, she was once again a most seaworthy vessel.

She went on to the Dunoon and Rothesay run, with an afternoon cruise to the Kyles of Bute thrown in, and with her stability regained was usually the L.N.E.R. winter boat.

In 1932 she was considerably altered internally. The main saloon was gutted, to be replaced by a combination of cocktail lounge, tea room and tiny alcove fitted with basket chairs—modern, but lacking the warmth of the older type saloon.

The year 1936 found the Craigendoran boats adopting a new livery of grey hulls and white upperworks and *Marmion* was one of the first to turn out in the new colour scheme. Although the Bute service was her customary route she made occasional jaunts to Loch Long and Loch Goil and in 1938 was a frequent visitor to Largs.

Marmion had a wonderfully placid existence as a pleasure craft. In all her years of service I recall only one incident out of the ordinary. This occurred in Rothesay Bay when she was lying out at the company moorings. She suffered the indignity of being rammed by a yacht and holed by its bowsprit, fortunately well above the waterline.

Taken for another spell of war duty in 1939 she was once again similarly reconstructed, but the good fortune that had attended her in the First World War now deserted her. She survived the holocaust of Dunkirk, where she added to the glory of the little ships, but was bombed and sunk at Harwich in April, 1941, in shallow water.

So passed from the scene the bonnie wee *Marmion*, the last vessel to join the fleet of the old North British Railway Company.

P.S. 'MARMION'

J. NICHOLSON.

P.S. Eagle III

IN 1910 the name *Eagle* cropped up again in Buchanan's fleet list, but this time suffixed by the Roman numeral III. The new boat was in actual fact the fourth *Eagle* to have been either built or bought for the company. In 1852 the first one appeared under the Buchanan houseflag and ran for 10 years before being sold for blockade running during the American Civil War. Number two was laid down to replace her but before she was launched the lure of gold proved too tempting and she, too, made her exit from the Clyde for the other side of the Atlantic. Only a year elapsed before the third was in the water and Buchanans had the use of her right up to 1892, when she went to the Manchester Ship Canal.

Eagle III was ordered from A. & J. Inglis, who subcontracted the building of the hull to Napier & Miller. Required for the all-the-way sailings, great speed was not imperative, nor were her internal decorations of the high standard of the crack railway boats of the period. An economical steamer capable of moderate pace was what Buchanan ordered and certainly *Eagle* was all that.

On the first day of June, 1910, the new ship duly appeared on the Clyde, sporting the black funnel with white band, but right from the start of her career it was apparent that there was a defect somewhere in her hull construction. With anything like a reasonable crowd aboard she listed to an alarming degree. As a result long before the season closed her name suddenly vanished from the Buchanan advertisements in the daily press . . . *Eagle* had gone back to the builders for modifications. She reappeared in 1911 completely cured of her ailment.

Long will she be remembered as the 11 o'clock boat from the Broomielaw for Dunoon, Rothesay and the Kyles of Bute with the full day's sail (including dinner and plain tea) at a cost of 4s. 6d. She alternated her Kyles cruise with ones to the head of Loch Striven or round the Island of Cumbrae.

The Admiralty claimed her for minesweeping work out of Grimsby and Harwich during the First World War and before she returned she was also engaged in conveying food between Britain and Holland.

As built, her navigating bridge had been placed between the paddleboxes but when reconditioned this was moved to forward of the funnel. A solid awning which covered part of her after deck was not replaced but in its stead there appeared a small upper deck over her after companionway.

By now the old Clyde firm of Buchanan had amalgamated with the equally well established one of Williamson and as a unit of the Williamson-Buchanan fleet *Eagle's* funnel colouring was changed to white with black top. The end of March, 1920, saw her back on her old route but the cost for the day's outing had doubled since before the war.

In 1933 she was ousted from her popular sailing time by the transference of the *King Edward* to the up-river fleet. Three years later the fleet had come under the Caledonian Steam Packet Company and *Eagle* appeared on a number of runs on railway connections at the coast termini. Later part of her weekly schedule was spent on the Loch Goil route.

She was conscripted again for white ensign work in the 1939-45 war and served as H.M.S. *Oriole*. During the Dunkirk evacuation she was grounded on the beach there, and thousands made their getaway via her decks while she acted the role of a temporary landing stage.

Eagle III was by no means a veteran, as Clyde steamers go, when she returned to her native river but her boiler was in need of replacement. The absence of a firm capable of producing the now outmoded haystack variety is said to have been the cause of her not returning to active Clyde service. After lying for some time in the Holy Loch she was towed to Port Glasgow and there broken up in 1946.

P.S. "EAGLE III"   J. NICHOLSON.

T.S. Duchess of Montrose

DENNY of Dumbarton launched a very notable vessel for the Clyde passenger fleet in 1930. She was given the title *Duchess of Montrose* and was the second steamer in the Caledonian Steam Packet Company to carry this name.

The former "Duchess" was a neat little paddleboat, built 28 years previously, and the new vessel, while greatly exceeding her forebear in tonnage, was likewise a distinguished looking craft.

Before the advent of the turbine *King George V* in 1926 all the members of the Clyde pleasure flotilla had their promenade decks open to the elements. The Williamson boat, however, had part of this deck enclosed to form an observation lounge and the *Duchess of Montrose* was also constructed on this pattern. Large windows made it a popular focal point with the passengers. As a result of this and other amenities, such as a cosy lounge below and a dining saloon on the main deck, the vessel was rated as a one class ship. No steerage fares were issued.

On trial her turbine machinery drove her at over 20 knots and altogether she was a worthwhile addition to the estuary.

If there was one blemish to mar her outline, it was the short pole mast aft, but this was heightened to full mainmast standard in 1934, though her looks might have been further enhanced had the builders been content with a foremast only.

Her home berth was at Gourock and her summer cruising took her to Ayr, round Arran and Ailsa Craig or on the ever popular "round the lochs" excursion. For a few years she even essayed the longer journey down to Stranraer.

During the years of war she was not called up to serve with the Royal Navy as were many of her sisters, but it was then that she probably experienced the most strenuous period of her career. Repainted, sometime in dark ochre upperworks and black hull, sometime all-over grey, she was based at Wemyss Bay, below the Cloch-Dunoon anti-submarine boom. From there she plied an almost continual four seasons ferry service to Rothesay, her after-deck often piled high with goods.

With the return of peace the *Duchess of Montrose* pursued a modified version of her pre-war cruising, with frequent voyages to Arran and Inveraray.

In May, 1945, the *King George V* (now a unit of the MacBrayne fleet) suffered a machinery defect and for a time the "Duchess" deputised for her on the Tarbert and Ardrishaig route.

The following year the Clyde experienced something of an Indian summer and in early October there was a one-day freak fog. Around Rothesay Bay and up river off Ashton the atmosphere was crystal clear but all along the Cowal shore the mist bank lurked dense and menacing.

On this particular day the *Duchess of Montrose* vanished into the murk on her afternoon run to Kirn, etc., but she failed to make the pier. Instead she embedded her bow on the rocky Cowal shore, so gently that few of her passengers were aware of her plight, but with sufficient force as to defy the combined efforts of her colleagues, the *King Edward, Duchess of Hamilton* and *Marchioness of Lorne*, to drag her clear. Tugs had to be called in to free her.

Under state control the "Duchess" deviated little in her post-war cruising, although more recently she has been a frequent visitor to Campbeltown.

In 1965, with the cut in the Clyde services, the *Duchess of Montrose* was laid up in Albert Harbour, Greenock, her finery dulling to drabness in the months of enforced idleness. As no reprieve was forthcoming, she was taken in tow to Ghent, there to await oblivion in the scrap yard.

T.S "DUCHESS OF MONTROSE"

J. NICHOLSON 1962.

P.S. Jeanie Deans

AT the beginning of 1923, the originators of the Craigendoran route to the coast, the North British, lost their identity in the London and North Eastern grouping in the railway amalgamations. The fleet remained unaltered for eight years before being enlarged by the addition of a new vessel, the *Jeanie Deans*. On April 7, 1931, a daughter of Mr. William Whitelaw, then chairman of the L.N.E.R., named the new boat at the Fairfield yard.

She was the second vessel to bear this name. Her predecessor, built almost half a century earlier, was one of the outstanding ships of her era and did much to bring the Craigendoran fleet to the forefront. The new vessel did nothing to besmirch that record. She was the biggest vessel to appear on this route—258 ft. long, 30 ft beam, 839 gross tons—and in her original guise sported two rather stumpy funnels which somehow did not altogether lend themselves to a ship of her length, smart though she undoubtedly looked. The shortness of the funnels was also the cause of much cinder being showered on her decks, unless the wind was blowing strongly from abeam. As a result " Jeanie " appeared in her second season with the " lums " heightened but unfortunately not to an equal degree. The cinder menace had been removed but aesthetically her outline had been sadly marred.

After war service *Jeanie Deans* reappeared in June, 1946, with yet another pair of funnels . . . elliptical and of greater girth and, it might be added, more in keeping with her dimensions.

As built, *Jeanie Deans'* promenade deck was almost completely unhampered but in 1932 she was given observation lounges fore and aft and these, after her spell on naval duty, were covered over to the full width of the vessel, although only the after one was allocated to passenger accommodation.

The L.N.E.R. retained the old N.B. livery of black hull, brown deck structures and red, white and black funnel. In 1936 there was a change when the hull became light grey and the deck buildings white.

Jeanie Deans sampled all these change and then donned the more austere colouring of the nationalised fleets in 1948.

The original after-saloon was a thing of beauty, with light oak woodwork and rose pink furnishings. This has since been converted into the main dining saloon previously located on a lower deck.

Plenty of power was evident in the engine room, where her three crank diagonal machinery drove her at a speed in excess of 18 knots on her trials, a pace which stamped her, like her predecessor, as one of the fastest paddle boats of her time.

The first duty of *Jeanie Deans* was on the Arrochar run in connection with the Loch Lomond tour. Then she essayed an assortment of cruises from Helensburgh and Craigendoran which took her to and round Arran, around Ailsa Craig, and to Ayr and Girvan.

After war service she was for a spell on the Kyles of Bute run, later on the round Bute cruise. She closed her Clyde career by alternating week about with the *Waverley* on the Arrochar and round Bute stations.

On war service she had been both minesweeper and anti-aircraft defence vessel and she narrowly escaped destruction during the London blitz from a land mine which accounted for the Clyde steamer *Juno*.

At the end of the 1964 season *Jeanie Deans* was laid up in Albert Harbour, Greenock, her services no longer required because of the policy of reduction in the Clyde flotilla. She was bought by a consortium of English businessmen who sailed her south. Her departure from the Clyde scene removed not only a popular paddle-boat but probably the best loved pleasure steamer of recent years.

Renamed *Queen of the South*, her service on the Thames has not been as successful as her days spent in Scottish waters.

PS. "JEANIE DEANS"   J. NICHOLSON.

T.S. Queen Mary II

THE departure of the paddle steamer *Isle of Arran* in the spring of 1933 did not for long leave a gap in the ranks of the Clyde up river fleet, for a ship of much greater tonnage was just about ready to replace the *Isle of Arran*, which went for service on the Thames.

The new ship was fitted out in Denny's yard and had been named *Queen Mary* on March 30. She is now the sole remaining Clyde pleasure boat to bear a regal title, once so popular. She was also the first turbine vessel to be constructed for the Bridge Wharf run and, if perhaps of not so fine a line as some of the Denny ships, is an extremely comfortable craft in which to travel.

The *Queen Mary* introduced some novel features in design on the Firth. Her cabin passengers were housed in the forepart of the ship and her boat deck extended right aft, almost to the stern, thus affording the steerage class not only a share of the top deck but also plenty of shelter without having to resort to the saloon below. Unlike the usual design of Clyde turbines she had a solid bulwark forward instead of an open rail and the passageway to her foredeck was via a stairway from the promenade deck instead of by the conventional doorway from the covered deck enclosures. The first class dining-saloon was also placed in the forepart of the vessel, while the second class contained a tearoom, sodabar, smokeroom and bar.

With a well raked mast just forward of the bridge, two heavily built funnels, a slightly raked stem and cruiser stern, the *Queen Mary* was an acquisition to the river fleet.

Under the command of Captain Donald McKinnon she took up the 10 o'clock run to Dunoon and Rothesay with a cruise to Largs and the coast of Arran as Williamson-Buchanan's biggest carrier. She became so popular with Glasgow day trippers that it was not uncommon to find her turning away passengers.

After two seasons there came a change, not in the affection of the travelling public, but in her title. The new Cunard liner, so long known simply as " 534 " at John Brown's of Clydebank, was at last ready for launching and her owners were most anxious to bestow on her the name *Queen Mary*, for Her Majesty was to perform the naming ceremony. As a gesture of goodwill the proprietors of the Clyde turbine made this possible by changing the name of their ship to *Queen Mary II*.

The addition of the Roman numeral to her name was the only change in her appearance and she continued to serve right up to the outbreak of war (her wonderful carrying capacity often being fully taxed in midsummer). By then she had come under L.M.S. control.

During the war years, with the Cloch-Dunoon boom in operation her activities were confined to the upper reaches of the Firth. She divided her time between service runs to the Cowal shore and the transportation of troops to and from the many liners which arrived in the Clyde with servicemen from overseas.

With Captain Fergus Murdoch now in command she reopened the postwar all-the-way sailings on June 1, 1946, and continued on this service after nationalisation.

During the war years she had appeared in various disguises of paintwork; battleship grey, black hull and upperworks in ochre, and towards the close of hostilities all-over light grey (almost silver in its pallor). The 1950s saw sweeping changes. A mainmast was added in 1954 and three years later, while being reboiled and converted to oil burning, her twin funnels were removed and a large, modern-looking oval one substituted.

In recent years the Bridge Wharf traffic has declined and only the *Queen Mary II* makes her way daily to Dunoon, Rothesay and the Kyles of Bute in the summer months (with the exception of Saturdays, when she is employed either on a cruise round Ailsa Craig or to Brodick).

The Clyde would be much the poorer without the presence of its last " royal lady," for she is now one of a meagre quartette of steam driven vessels remaining on Clyde waters.

T. S. "QUEEN MARY II"

J. NICHOLSON

P.S. Caledonia

DENNY of Dumbarton turned out in 1934 their first paddle steamer for the Clyde passenger fleet since they had launched the famous *Duchess of Hamilton* in 1890. The reason for the new tonnage was the departure to the breakers of two old faithfuls, the *Caledonia* and the *Mercury*, which had figured in the original building programmes of the Caledonian and Glasgow and South Western fleets respectively.

The replacements were also paddle driven and assumed the same titles, but here the similarity ended. In external design the new *Caledonia* (and her quasi-sister the *Mercury* building at Fairfield) were revolutionary types for the river. They had twin masts, elliptical funnels, observation lounges on the promenade deck with passenger accommodation atop, and flying bridges which protruded beyond the breadth of the hulls. Cruiser sterns were also adopted.

Perhaps the most startling change was in the design of the paddle-boxes. Gone were the lovely curve offline and the symmetrical vents and decorative embellishments. In their place there was a rectangular box-like affair on deck while the choke escapes were spaced apart like saloon windows. Indeed it was somewhat difficult to distinguish the new craft as "sidewheelers" when viewing them from a distance on the beam.

Below deck was another novelty; the cabin dining saloon was placed in the position normally occupied by the saloon. Below that there was a tea room and smoke room. With a capacity of 1,300 passengers, the *Caledonia* was a roomy, comfortable and most efficient vessel.

After topping 17 knots on the Skelmorlie mile, the *Caledonia* came into service on March 31, the Saturday of the Glasgow Spring Holiday and special handbills were produced to entice the travelling public to sample the new boats on their initial runs. The *Caledonia* was on the Gourock and Wemyss Bay connections to Dunoon, Rothesay and the Kyles and proved herself a worthy vessel.

During the ensuing summer she ran short cruises from Largs and Millport and in her first off-season helped out with the winter services. Two years later she replaced the *Duchess of Argyll* in summer on the Arran route via the Kyles of Bute and was quite often seen up-river at week-ends on cruises from Bridge Wharf.

The *Caledonia* was commissioned for war service in December, 1939, and played her part as minesweeper and flak ship in the Dover Patrol, the Battle of Britain, the Normandy D-Day landings, the relief of Antwerp and the Battle of the V Bombs. On Christmas Eve, 1940, she was on patrol with the *Mercury* off the south-east corner of Ireland when the latter hit a mine. For four hours the *Caledonia* laboured to tow the stricken ship back to port but the *Mercury* sank some miles out from Milford Haven.

The *Caledonia* arrived back on the Clyde in May, 1945, but it was 12 months before she resumed her peace-time duties.

Since her return she has played many roles on the Clyde coast scene. She has made railway connections from all the coastal terminii, done the Arran and Campbeltown cruises as well as the trip round the Island of Bute and was the excursion steamer from Ayr for a time.

The *Caledonia* was the first of the Clyde paddlers to be converted to oil burning when the Railway Executive decided to adopt this fuel. (Back in the 'nineties Captain Williamson had tried oil fuel in her predecessor but with mixed results and she was soon back on coal.)

Not all the exciting episodes of Caledonia's career were confined to the war years. Before she donned navy grey she and the *Duchess of Argyll* were in collision at Gourock. Then in December, 1953, her engines broke down off Innellan on the 10.25 morning up run from Rothesay and she had to drop anchor. A tug eventually towed her to Wemyss Bay. Of recent years she has had a more tranquil existence, though on one occasion the *Glen Sannox* had to come to her assistance when she had an engine failure in Millport Bay.

D.E.P.V. "TALISMAN" in 1935.

J. NICHOLSON.

P.S. Jupiter

SOMETHING new in profile was added to the Clyde scene in 1937 when the Fairfield yard launched from the same slipway two almost identical paddleboats for the London Midland and Scottish fleet. These were the *Juno* (lost in the London blitz of 1941) and the *Jupiter*.

This pair were given deck observation lounges, concealed type paddleboxes and twin masts, features which had been introduced during this decade, but unlike the other paddleboats of the flotilla they sported two funnels.

Of pleasing design in spite of the attempt to disguise the fact that she was a paddle steamer, *Jupiter* somehow never quite attained the speed of her twin. She was, nevertheless, with her great beam and space amidships a grand passenger and goods carrier and a most useful member of the fleet.

Her career began on the Dunoon-Rothesay-Kyles of Bute service and after an uneventful opening spell she ran into trouble while on her first winter duty. In attempting to take Millport (not always the most pleasant of tasks in wintertime) she was caught by the southerly swell and rammed the pier to a depth of several feet. When in the following June she was in collision with several yachts moored off Hunter's Quay one would be tempted to believe that she was rather slow in answering to the helm. Her episodes extraordinary were not concluded until she had gone ashore near Brodick during a particularly thick fog.

Having got over her youthful adventures she settled down and was one of the first vessels to be called to Admiralty duty in the war. As H.M.S. *Scawfell* she served with distinction as a minesweeper in the Clyde area and later at Milford Haven, Portland and Dover. After a period as an anti-aircraft unit on the east coast convoy routes she was in the thick of the battle during the Normandy landings.

She was the first Clyde steamer to return to peace-time work and went on to the Holy Loch run in February, 1946. During the summer she returned to give a modified version of her Dunoon and Rothesay trading. When the car ferries made their debut *Jupiter* was relegated to the role of assistant steamer on the Wemyss Bay-Rothesay run. She also became identified with the Cumbrae Circle Cruise and made occasional sailings from Ayr and from the Bridge Wharf to Lochgoil.

Having been converted from coal burning to oil fuel early in 1957 it was rather surprising to find her taken out of service and laid up in Albert Harbour, Greenock, the same year. Finally in April, 1961, she departed for the shipbreakers in Dublin. So passed just about the most pleasing design of the dwindling Clyde paddle fleet.

R.M.S. "COLUMBA"   J. NICHOLSON

P.S. Ivanhoe

PASSENGERS who imbibed well rather than wisely became something of a problem on the Clyde river steamers in the 19th century, so much so that in the 1870's a consortium of businessmen decided to run a vessel on strictly teetotal lines. They formed the Frith of Clyde Steam Packet Company and on February 25, 1880, a 225-foot long paddle steamer was launched at the yard of D. and W. Henderson. She was given the name *Ivanhoe* and although she made her headquarters at Helensburgh she was not connected with the North British fleet then based there. After the launch the guests were entertained by the builders in the model-room at Meadowside, when a rather incongruous note was struck by the speeches being toasted in wine!

The *Ivanhoe* was a twin funnel saloon steamer, typical of the period, with narrow alleyways running down the outside of the main and fore saloons. The normal refreshment bars, however, were conspicuous by their absence. On May 3 she underwent her trials and at the beginning of June went into service. On her opening cruise she encountered both the *Glen Rosa* and the *Sheila* on the route to Arran when, sad to relate, the new ship came off worst.

Her daily run was by way of Greenock Custom House Quay, Princes Pier, Kirn, Dunoon, Wemyss Bay, Rothesay, Tighnabruaich, Corrie and Brodick to Lamlash. On Mondays, Wednesdays, and Fridays she extended her voyage to King's Cross and Whiting Bay. During her first season a special extra run was made on Saturdays either to Campbeltown, round Arran or round Ailsa Craig. Later on Pladda was the objective of the extra sail and still later gave way to an evening cruise, a form of excursion which this steamer inaugurated and popularised.

Another new steamer, the *Scotia*, had to deputise for the *Ivanhoe* in the first week of her service as the *Ivanhoe* broke down after leaving Wemyss Bay and had to be towed into Rothesay by the steam yacht *Matador*. Her first two seasons, however, were so successful that in September, 1881, the local press carried a report that four Clyde yards had been asked to estimate for building three more steamers to expand the Firth of Clyde Company's business.

Under the command of Captain James Williamson, who was also part owner, the *Ivanhoe* continued to prosper (although she did not get any additional fleet units to assist her). Captain Williamson left her at the close of the decade to become Marine Superintendent of the new Caledonian Steam Packet Company.

In the spring of 1894 the *Ivanhoe* went south for the opening of the Manchester Ship Canal but was back in her native waters for the start of the summer season. Three years later she was bought outright by the C.S.P. Company—although to all intents and purposes she had been plying under their supervision for some time—and bars were installed.

Her new owners placed her on ordinary coast connections from the railway termini and she was no longer regarded as a cruise boat. The year 1911 found her again changing hands, this time on the Broomielaw run, for a firm known as the Firth of Clyde Steam Packet Company. They changed her yellow funnels to white and later added narrow black tops. By 1914 she was in the hands of Turbine Steamers Limited, who lengthened the black funnel tops to the conventional depth. She was running frequently to Lochgoilhead at this time but when the war curtailed the sailings she was chartered to the Caledonian company and once again became a railway boat. At first she ran from Rothesay to Wemyss Bay but later was engaged solely above the Dunoon-Cloch boom on the Gourock, Kirn, Dunoon station.

In 1920 the *Ivanhoe* was handed back to Turbine Steamers but lay in harbour at Greenock until she made the sad passage to the breaker's yard at Dumbarton.

P.S. "JUPITER"   J. NICHOLSON

M.V. Maid of Skelmorlie

THE withdrawal of such big ships as *Duchess of Argyll* and *King Edward* from the Clyde fleet left a gap that was filled by four vessels—the " Maids ".

Mid-February of 1953 saw the first of the " Quads," the *Maid of Ashton*. in the water, followed by the *Maid of Argyll*. On April 2 *Maid of Skelmorlie* was launched at the Pointhouse yard of Messrs. A. and J. Inglis. By June 22 she was on the Skelmorlie mile registering 15 knots and in service three days later. *Maid of Cumbrae* was the last to be launched.

Maid of Skelmorlie, like her three sisters, was an innovation in Clyde steamer circles; in fact she was not a steamer at all, being driven by a pair of Polar diesel engines. The bow was high and slanting, the stern low set. A full sweep of promenade deck right from the bridge almost to the stern was devoid of any obstruction and gave passengers ample opportunity of viewing the passing scene. Forward, the bridge, wheelhouse and stored life saving equipment blocked the view.

A somewhat squat funnel could have done with more height to enhance her outline, as would the fitting of one mast instead of two in a ship of her length, only 165 feet. During construction, however, new lighting regulations, necessitating the carrying of a second mast, were introduced.

Below decks the ample seating accommodation was utilitarian compared with the comfortable saloons of paddle steamer days. Row after row of fixed seats, all facing forward, gave the appearance of a miniature cinema or bingo hall, and from the front seats the view forward was completely obscured by the high bulwarks.

Noise and vibration were much more pronounced than in steam driven vessels, but the " Maids " were handy little ships with plenty of power and manoeuvrability. All the masters who have commanded them speak highly of their excellent sea qualities. To begin with, some regular voyagers were doubtful, but in late October, 1953, they got their answer. In the first taste of really dirty weather, *Maid of Skelmorlie* was on the evening run to Rothesay. She made excellent time and came through with flying colours.

Maid of Skelmorlie's duties have been many and varied since she came to join the Clyde fleet—railway connections, cruising, tendering and charter parties—while each winter she has taken her share of the off-season sailings. She was the first of her class to don the new blue livery of the Caledonian Steam Packet Company on her hull but the red lions on her funnel did not appear until another six months had elapsed. She was the last Clyde vessel to call at Lochgoilhead before that pier was closed to passenger traffic in July, 1965.

In the earlier years of her existence most of the *Skelmorlie's* work has been on the Largs, Rothesay and Millport sections. Included was that innovation to the waters of the Firth of Clyde, the " Cafe Cruise," when the addition of a cup of coffee and a chocolate biscuit was coupled with two hours' cruising without extra cost.

Of recent years she has not been allocated any special run for the summer months but has taken her turn with the *Maid of Argyll* and *Maid of Cumbrae* on a three-weekly rota. During the 1967 season this duty was extended to one in every four weeks since the *Maid of Ashton* was able to join the group, having been relieved on the Holy Loch service by the *Countess of Breadalbane*.

One drawback of the " Maid " class is their inability to cope with capacity crowds at the peak of the holiday season and many a time a good old-fashioned paddlesteamer, with her spacious decks, has been called in to render assistance.

M.V. "MAID OF SKELMORLIE"

J. NICHOLSON.

M.V. Glen Sannox

WITH the upsurge in car ownership since the 1930's the coming of the car ferry was inevitable, delayed without a doubt by the Second World War.

The earliest record of a vehicle being transported by Clyde steamer (though probably by no means the first) is to be found in the daily press of 1877. A collision between the Arran steamers *Glen Rosa* and *Guinevere* resulted in the appearance of the two masters at the River Bailie's Court. There it was revealed that the *Guinevere* at the time of the incident was carrying a horse and carriage on her decks. The violence of the collision caused the animal to take fright and attempt to bolt, while the carriage burst its tethering bonds.

Twenty years after this episode the first motor car was landed at Rothesay from the Williamson steamer *Strathmore* by means of gang planks from her deck on to the pier. This primitive and often dangerous mode of disembarkation was in vogue on the Clyde for more than half a century.

In 1939 the L.M.S. considered the introduction of a specially designed ferry capable of accommodating 27 cars but the outbreak of war upset the plan and it was late in 1952 before an order was placed. By the following September the first vessel, *Arran*, had been launched and she was soon followed by two sister ships, *Cowal* and *Bute*. The introduction of collapsible bulwarks and mechanically operated lifts permitted vehicles to be handled with comparative speed at any state of the tide and the three ships were soon giving a frequent service to Dunoon and Rothesay from the mainland.

So successful were these craft, both on service and as money earners, that in March, 1956, an enlarged version was ordered for the Arran route. She was launched on the last day of April, 1957, at Troon, the naming ceremony being performed by Mrs. J. Ness, wife of the General Manager of British Railways (Scottish Region). The new vessel was the *Glen Sannox*, the third to bear this title. As both the former ships had been outstanding, the new recipient had a high standard to maintain.

Glen Sannox (the third) is 238 feet in length with a beam and gross tonnage in excess of any of her predecessors. She has accommodation for 1,000 passengers and 40 cars (60 if no cargo is carried).

Her designed speed of 17½ knots is derived from two Sulzer marine diesel engines.

First impressions varied. The Arran people in the main deemed her '' a worthy ship,'' but to those who could recall the two former holders of the name she suffered greatly in appearance. They had both been outstandingly handsome ships; sleek greyhounds capable of over 20 knots. One critic of the new ship likened her appearance to ''. . . a tub with a tenement aboard for ballast.''

June 29, 1957, found *Glen Sannox* making her first crossing from Ardrossan to Brodick, six days ahead of her scheduled maiden trip. The terminal pier on Arran had been strengthened to take the weight of the new boat which, because of her bulk, is not suitable for going alongside the smaller piers of the Firth. She rarely deviates from the Ardrossan-Brodick-Fairlie circuit, though she has visited Rothesay and has made a special call at Largs to take cargo aboard.

In August of her first season she had teething trouble with her car lift as a result of which *Bute* was despatched down the Firth to take over her duties. Some difficulty was also experienced at Fairlie, where other vessels found access to the pier troublesome because of the girth of the new Arran boat.

In her second year of service she exhibited her sea-going qualities when extreme autumnal gales disrupted and even halted shipping all over the estuary. With the most exposed section to cross she ploughed her way through the worst of the storm, arriving at Brodick on her evening run over four hours behind schedule. She began taking on vehicles for the mainland around 11 p.m., reaching Fairlie at 1 a.m. She then turned about and battled her way back to the shelter of Brodick Bay for what was left of the night.

Some years afterwards *Glen Sannox* again proved her worth by going to the rescue of *Caledonia* which had broken down and was in a perilous position within the confines of Millport Bay.

Like all the car ferries of the Clyde, *Glen Sannox* is the answer to the motorist's prayer but the gangway exits for passengers leave much to be desired. Certainly no beauty, the *Glen Sannox* is still a roomy and comfortable ship and ideally suited to the task for which she was constructed.

M.V. 'GLEN SANNOX'

J. NICHOLSON

List of Vessels in Service on the Clyde, 1900—1967

AILSA—Steam, screw, single funnel, lgth. 75 ft. Blt. 1906 Ailsa Shipbuilding Co., Troon, for M. Girvan Service: Cruising from Girvan to Ailsa Craig. Sold 1924 for service on Cromarty Firth.

AILSA—Steam, screw, single funnel, lgth. 95 ft. Blt. 1924 Ailsa Shipbuilding Co., Ayr, for Mr. Girvan's service to Ailsa Craig. Renamed *Lady Ailsa*. Sold to France, 1932.

ARDYNE—Steam, screw, single funnel, lgth. 135 ft. Blt. 1928 Scott & Sons, Bowling, for Clyde Cargo Steamers. Various cargo and limited passenger services from Glasgow to coast. Broken up Troon 1955.

ARRAN—Steam, screw, single funnel, lgth. 110 ft. Blt. 1879 J. Fullerton & Co., Paisley. Acquired by Hill & Co., for cargo and limited passenger accommodation between Glasgow and the coast. Sold 1917 to J. Boyle, Glasgow.

ARRAN—Steam, screw, single funnel, lgth. 99 ft. Blt. 1926 Ayrshire Dockyard Co., Irvine, for Clyde Cargo Steamers. Cargo and limited passenger service Glasgow to coast. Wrecked Loch Fyne 1933.

ARRAN—Steam, screw, single funnel, lgth. 120 ft. Blt. 1933 Ardrossan Drydock Co., for Clyde Cargo Steamers. Limited passenger accommodation and cargo runs from Glasgow to coast. Renamed *Kildonan*. Broken up Port Glasgow 1958.

ARRAN—Motor, screw, single funnel, lgth. 179 ft. Blt. 1953 Denny Bros., Dumbarton, for CSPC. First car ferry in the Clyde fleet and still in service.

ARRAN MAIL—Motor, screw, single funnel, lgth. 95 ft. Blt. 1936 Denny Bros., Dumbarton, for CSPC. Cargo and limited passenger accommodation. Service Ardrossan to Arran. Sold 1951 to Channel Islands.

ASHTON—Motor, screw, no funnel, lgth. 63 ft. Blt. 1938 Denny Bros., Dumbarton, for CSPC. During Empire Exhibition ran trips from Broomielaw to view Cunarder *Queen Elizabeth* building at Clydebank. For many years on the Largs/Millport run. Sold 1964 to Messrs. Ritchie for ferry service between Gourock and Kilcreggan.

ATALANTA—Steam, screw, single funnel, lgth, 210 ft. Blt. 1906 John Brown, Clydebank for G. & S.W.R., their only turbine steamer. Services mainly out of Ardrossan to Arran. Served with R.N. 1914/18. Sold to Blackpool 1937.

BENMORE—Steam, paddle, single funnel, lgth. 201 ft. Blt. 1876 T. Seath & Co., Rutherglen for Capt. R. Campbell's Glasgow to Holy Loch service. Had various owners thereafter and had two funnels for short period. Chartered by CSPC during 1914-18 war. On fire Greenock Harbour 1920, scrapped Dumbarton 1923.

BUTE—Steam, screw, single funnel, lgth. 110 ft. Blt. 1892 J. Fullerton & Co., Paisley for Hill & Co. Cargo and limited passenger accommodation. Service Glasgow to various Clyde ports. Sold 1901.

BUTE—Motor, screw, single funnel, lgth. 179 ft. Blt. 1954 Ailsa Shipbuilding Co., Troon for CSPC for passenger and motor car ferry duties from Gourock or Wemyss Bay. Still in service.

BUTE 4—Steam, screw, single funnel, lgth. 115 ft. Blt. 1898 J. Fullerton & Co., Paisley for Hill & Co. Various Clyde routes from Glasgow with cargo and limited number of passengers. Broken up Ardrossan 1935.

CALEDONIA—Steam, paddle, single funnel, lgth. 200 ft. Blt. 1889 J. Reid & Co., Port Glasgow. Original vessel launched for the CSPC Rothesay and Millport service, from Gourock and Wemyss Bay, and latterly long association with Gourock-Holy Loch run. Broken up Barrow 1933.

CALEDONIA (1934)—See page 42.

CAVALIER—Steam, paddle, single funnel, lgth. 151 ft. Blt. 1883 Aitken & Mansell, Glasgow for D. MacBrayne. Normally on W. Highland services but in certain seasons acted as feeder from Glasgow to Greenock for *Iona's* sailings. Sold 1919 to N. of Scotland, Orkney & Shetland Steam Navig. Co.

CARRICK LASS—Motor, screw, no funnel, lgth. 57 ft. Blt. 1934 H. McLean, Govan for M. Greig, Girvan. Girvan to Ailsa Craig cruises. Sold to Southampton.

CHANCELLOR—Steam, paddle, single funnel, lgth. 199 ft. Blt. 1880 R. Chambers, Dumbarton for Loch Lomond Co. and based at Helensburgh for a while, on service to Arrochar. Sold to Lochgoil and Lochlong Steamboat Co., and later to G & SWR. Sold to Spain 1901.

CHEVALIER—Steam, paddle, twin funnels, lgth. 211 ft. Blt. 1886 J. & G. Thomson, Clydebank, for David Hutcheson & Co. (later MacBrayne). On W. Highland routes but winter boat to Ardrishaig for many years. Wrecked Loch Fyne 1927 and broken up at Troon.

CLYDESDALE—Steam, screw, single funnel, lgth. 151 ft. Blt. 1905 Scott & Sons, Bowling, for D. MacBrayne. Service almost entirely in W. Highland waters but rare appearances on feeder run from Glasgow to Greenock. Scrapped Port Glasgow 1953.

COLUMBA—See page 6.

COMET—Motor, screw, no funnel, lgth 65 ft. Blt. 1905 by A. W. Robertson & Co., and running under name *Win* in English waters. Bought by D. MacBrayne 1907 and renamed *Comet*. After spell on W. Coast routes became Loch Goil mail boat for 30 years. Sold to Shoreham 1947 and now known as *Gradely*.

COUNTESS OF BREADALBANE—Motor, screw, no funnel, lgth. 90 ft. Blt. 1936 Denny Bros., Dumbarton, for CSPC services on Loch Awe. Taken from loch 1952 and transported overland to Loch Fyne to join Clyde fleet. Associated principally with Largs-Millport run but now on Holy Loch service from Gourock.

COWAL—Steam, screw, single funnel, lgth. 135 ft. Blt. 1903 Scott & Sons, Bowling, for David MacBrayne and named *Lapwing*. Served outside the Firth of Clyde, sold for work in Channel and Scilly Isles, brought back to Clyde 1920 by Clyde Cargo Steamers and renamed *Cowal*. Cargo and limited passenger accommodation between Glasgow and the coast. Scrapped 1931.

COWAL—Motor, screw, single funnel, lgth. 179 ft. Blt. 1954 Ailsa Shipbuilding Co., Troon, for C.S.P.C. Passenger and motor car ferry duties from Gourock or Wemyss Bay. Still in service.

CYGNET—Steam, screw, single funnel, lgth. 135 ft. Blt. 1904 A. & J. Inglis, Pointhouse, Glasgow, for MacBrayne. Mainly cargo but limited passenger accommodation, Glasgow to Inveraray run. Transferred to W. Highland waters after 1914-18 war. Broken up Barrow 1931.

CULZEAN CASTLE (1895)—See page 24.

DALRIADA—Steam, screw, single funnel, lgth. 230 ft. Blt. 1926 R. Duncan & Co., Port Glasgow, for Campbeltown & Glasgow Steam Packet Co., for service from Glasgow to Kintyre. Taken over by Admiralty as salvage vessel and lost in Thames Estuary 1942.

DANDIE DINMONT—Steam, paddle, single funnel, lgth. 195 ft. (later lengthened to 209 ft.). Blt. 1895 A. & J. Inglis, Pointhouse, for NB services from Craigendoran. Transferred 1928 to LNER Humber ferry service and renamed *Frodingham*.

DAVAAR—See page 12.

DIANA VERNON—Steam, paddle, single funnel, lgth. 180 ft. Blt. 1885 Barclay Curle & Co., for Holy Loch and Gareloch services from Craigendoran for N.B. Sold 1901 to Brighton owners and renamed *Worthing Belle*.

DUCHESS OF ARGYLL—Steam, screw, twin funnels, lgth. 250 ft. Blt. 1906 Denny Bros., Dumbarton, for CSPC. Their first turbine, making over 21 knots. After initial service on Ardrossan/Arran run became associated Gourock to Arran route via Kyles of Bute for many years. Later duties varied. Troopship in 1914-18 war, sold to Admiralty 1952 and hull moored in Portland Harbour as floating laboratory.

DUCHESS OF FIFE (1903)—See page 30.

DUCHESS OF HAMILTON (1890)—See page 18.

DUCHESS OF HAMILTON—Steam, screw, twin funnels, lgth. 262 ft. Blt. 1932 Harland & Wolff Ltd., Govan, for CSPC. Speed over 20 knots. Pre-war duties assortment of cruises out of Ayr, since then on Gourock/Campbeltown run and taking on additional cruises as Clyde fleet was reduced in number. Still in service.

DUCHESS OF MONTROSE—Steam, paddle, single funnel, lgth. 210 ft. Blt. 1902 John Brown & Co., Clydebank, for CSPC railway connections from Gourock and Wemyss Bay. Mined off Belgian coast 1917.

DUCHESS OF MONTROSE (1930)—See page 36.

DUCHESS OF ROTHESAY—Steam, paddle, single funnel, lgth. 225 ft. Blt. 1895 J. & G. Thomson, Clydebank, for CSPC. During long career served out of Gourock, Wemyss Bay and Ardrossan. Very fast. Taken over by Admiralty during both world wars but did not return from latter. Broken up in Holland.

DUCHESS OF YORK (1884)—See *Isle of Cumbrae*.

EAGLE III (1910)—See page 34.

EDINBURGH CASTLE—Steam, paddle, single funnel, lgth. 205 ft. Blt. 1879 R. Duncan & Co., Port Glasgow, for Lochgoil and Inveraray Steam Packet Co. On service throughout entire career from Glasgow to Lochgoilhead. Outstanding because of enormous paddleboxes. Taken over by Turbine Steamers Ltd., 1912. Broken up 1913.

FAIR MAID—Steam, paddle, single funnel, lgth. 235 ft. Built 1915 A. & J. Inglis, Pointhouse, Glasgow, for NB services from Craigendoran. Conscripted by Admiralty before she could take her place in fleet and sunk by mine 1916.

FUSILIER—Steam, paddle, single funnel, lgth. 202 ft. Blt. 1888 McArthur & Co., Paisley, for D. MacBrayne. Clipper bow and bowsprit. On varied W. Highland services but chartered to CSPC for Clyde duties during first war. For three seasons in 1920's was Ardishaig winter boat. Sold to Redcliffe Shipping Co. 1934 for service in Firth of Forth. After assuming different owners and names south of the Border was scrapped at Barrow 1939.

GAEL—Steam, paddle, twin funnels, lgth. 211 ft. Blt. 1867 Robertson & Co., Greenock, for Campbetown & Glasgow Steam Packet Co. Purchased 1891 by D. MacBrayne and placed on on varying W. Highland routes. In Clyde service to Ardishaig at close of 1914-18 war and during war also on Ardrossan/Arran run. Sold for scrapping 1924.

GALATEA—Steam, paddle, twin funnels, lgth. 230 ft. Blt. 1889 Caird & Co., for CSPC. On various railway connections and cruises from Gourock and Wemyss Bay. Sold to Italy 1906.

GLENCOE—Steam, paddle, single funnel, lgth. 149 ft. (lengthened to 165 ft.). Blt. 1846 Tod & McGregor, Glasgow, for Stornoway owner and named *Mary Jane*. Eventually passed into Hutcheson (later MacBrayne) hands and was renamed *Glencoe*. Saw service in Clyde during 1914-18 war and in early twenties. Broken up Ardrossan 1931.

GLEN ROSA (1893)—See page 22.

GLEN SANNOX—Steam, paddle, twin funnels, lgth. 260 ft. Blt. 1892 J. & G. Thomson, Clydebank, for G & SWR. Fastest paddle steamer on Firth of Clyde, over 20 knots. Mainly on Ardrossan/Arran route. Returned by Admiralty as unsuitable for war work, came under LMS control and broken up Port Glasgow 1925.

GLEN SANNOX—Steam, screw, twin funnels, lgth. 249 ft. Blt. 1925 Denny Bros., for LMS to replace paddlesteamer of same name on Ardrossan/Arran route. Over 21 knots. Sold for scrapping in Belgium 1954.

GLEN SANNOX (1957)—See page 50.

GRENADIER (1885)—See page 10.

HEATHER BELL—Steam, paddle, single funnel, lgth. 207 ft. Blt. 1871 Blackwood & Gordon, Port Glasgow, for Duke of Hamilton's Trustees. On Ardrossan/Arran service. Sold to south coast 1873 but came back to Clyde for 1900 season under charter. Broken up 1903.

IONA—Steam, paddle, twin funnels, lgth. 255 ft. Blt. 1864 J. & G. Thomson, Clydebank, for Hutchesons (later MacBrayne's) fleet. Lengthy service on Ardishaig, Lochgoilhead and W. Highland runs before being broken up at Dalmuir in 1936.

ISLE OF ARRAN—Steam, paddle, single funnel, lgth. 210 ft. Blt. 1892 T. Seath, Rutherglen, for Buchanan Steamers Glasgow to Arran run, minesweeper in war. Sold 1933 to GSN Co. for service on Thames. Scrapped 1936.

ISLE OF BUTE—Steam, paddle, single funnel, lgth. 205 ft. Blt. 1877 Caird & Co., Greenock, for Campbell & Gillies and named *Sheila*. Bought by NB and renamed *Guy Mannering*. In 1894 purchased by Buchanan Steamers and changed name to *Isle of Bute*. On Broomielaw to Rothesay route. Sold to Morecambe 1912, broken up 1913.

ISLE OF CUMBRAE—Steam, paddle, single funnel, lgth. 210 ft. Blt. 1884 as *Jeanie Deans* by Barclay Curle & Co., Glasgow, for NB express service from Craigendoran. Said to be fastest vessel in Clyde service for many years. Originally a flush deck design. Sold to Londonderry owners but returned to Clyde as *Duchess of York*. Bought by Buchanan Steamers 1904 and renamed *Isle of Cumbrae*. On day cruises from Broomielaw. During 1914-18 war on charter to G & SWR. Broken up Dumbarton 1921.

ISLE OF SKYE—See Madge Wildfire.

JEANIE DEANS (1931)—See page 38.

IVANHOE (1880)—See page 8.

JUNO (1898)—See page 26.

JUNO—Steam, paddle, twin funnels, lgth. 231 ft. Blt. 1937 Fairfield, Govan, for LMS connections to the coast. As HMS *Helvellyn* acted as minesweeper and A-A escort vessel during war. Sunk by bombs in London Docks 1941.

JUPITER—Steam, paddle, single funnel, lgth. 230 ft. Blt. 1896 J. & G. Thomson, Clydebank, for G & SWR services from Princes Pier. Very fast. Early years spent on Arran route via the Kyles of Bute. Minesweeper 1914-18 war. Scrapped Barrow 1935.

JUPITER (1937)—See page 46.

KENILWORTH—Steam, paddle, single funnel, lgth. 215 ft. Blt. 1898 A. & J. Inglis, Pointhouse, for NB express service to coast via Craigendoran. Very fast. War service as minesweeper, withdrawn at end of 1937 season and scrapped in yard in which she was built.

KEPPEL—Motor, screw, exhaust up mast-cum-funnel, lgth. 110 ft. Blt. 1961 White's Shipyard, Southampton, as Rose for Tilbury-Gravesend ferry service, transferred to CSPC 1967 and renamed Keppel. Placed on Largs/Millport route. Still in service.

KING EDWARD (1901)—See page 26.

KING GEORGE V—Steam, screw, twin funnels, lgth. 260 ft. Blt. 1926 Denny Bros., Dumbarton, for Turbine Steamers Greenock to Campbeltown or Inveraray. First Clyde steamer with enclosed promenade deck. Transferred to David Mac-Brayne 1936 and placed on Oban/Staffa/Iona cruise. Helped in Dunkirk evacuation. Still based at Oban in summer but makes occasional appearances on Ardrishaig route off season.

KINLOCH—Steam, screw, single funnel, lgth. 206 ft. Blt. 1878 A. & J. Inglis, Pointhouse, for Campbeltown & Glasgow Steam Packet Co. Clipper bow and bowsprit. Service between Glasgow and Campbeltown. Sold to Channel Islands 1926. Broken up Bo'ness 1928.

KINTYRE—Steam, screw, single funnel, lgth. 184 ft. Blt. 1868 Robertson, Port Glasgow, for Campbeltown and Glasgow SPC. Service Glasgow to Campbeltown. Clipper bow and bowsprit. Sunk in collision off Skelmorlie 1907.

KYLEMORE—Steam, paddle, single funnel, lgth. 200 ft. Bldg. 1897 Russell & Co., Port Glasgow, for John Williamson but sold before completion to south of England firm and renamed Britannia. Brought back to Clyde 1904 and as unit of G & SW fleet running as Vulcan usually out of Fairlie. 1908 reverted to John Williamson and her first name. Minesweeping first war and as netlayer in second. Bombed and sunk at Harwich 1940.

LADY AILSA—Motor, screw, no funnel, lgth. 52 ft. Blt. 1934 H. McLean & Sons, Govan, for Mr Girvan's cruises to Ailsa Craig from Girvan.

LADY CLARE—Steam, paddle, single funnel, lgth. 180 ft. Blt. 1891 J. McArthur & Co., Paisley, for NB services from Craigendoran to Gareloch-head and Princess Pier. 1906 sold for service on Lough Foyle. Minesweeper in war. Broken up Dumbarton 1928.

LADY OF THE ISLES—Steam, paddle, twin funnels, lgth. 246 ft. Blt. 1877 D. & W. Henderson, Glasgow, as Lord of the Isles for Glasgow & Inveraray Steeamboat Co., service Glasgow to Inveraray. Sold 1890 to Thames, later renamed Jupiter. Returned to Clyde 1904 for Isles Steamship Co. and renamed Lady of the Isles, sailing from Broomielaw to coast. Broken up Dumbarton 1905.

LADY ROWENA—Steam, paddle, single funnel, lgth. 200 ft. Blt. 1891 S. McKnight & Co., Ayr, for NB service from Craigendoran to Arrochar. Sold to Italy 1903, but returned to Clyde via service at Newhaven, 1911, for Captain Cameron's excursions from Glasgow to the coast. Minesweeping service in war. Sold thereafter to English owners and broken up 1922.

LEVEN—Motor, screw, no funnel, lgth. 63 ft. Blt. 1938 Denny Bros., Dumbarton, for CSPC. During Empire Exhibition at Glasgow that year ran cruises from Bridge Wharf to view Cunarder Queen Elizabeth building at Clydebank. For many years on Largs/Millport run. Sold 1964 to Ireland.

LOCHFYNE—Motor, screw, twin funnels, lgth. 209 ft. Blt. 1931 Denny Bros., Dumbarton, for David MacBrayne's summer service from Oban to Staffa and Iona. Winter Ardrishaig mail boat, also used on Oban/Fort William run. On Clyde during war years. On withdrawal of Saint Columba has taken over Loch Fyne sailing. Still in service.

LOCHIEL—Motor, screw, single funnel, lgth. 183 ft. Blt. 1939 Denny Bros., Dumbarton, for David MacBrayne's services outwith the Clyde. On relief duties to Ardrishaig in the 1940's. Still in service out of West Loch Tarbert.

LOCHINVAR—Motor, screw, single funnel, lgth. 145 ft. Blt. 1908 Scott & Sons, Bowling, for David MacBrayne. Service Oban/Tobermory run. In 1940's relieved on Loch Goil run. Sold 1960 to Thames and renamed Anzio I. Lost off East Coast en route to Cromarty Firth 1966.

LOCHNESS—Steam, screw, single funnel, lgth. 200 ft. Blt. 1929 Harland & Wolff, Govan, for David MacBrayne's Mallaig to Stornoway run. Before taking up this duty helped on Ardrishaig route in Glasgow Fair Week 1929. Sold to Italy 1955.

LOCHNEVIS—Motor, screw, single funnel, lgth. 175 ft. Blt. 1934 Denny Bros., Dumbarton, for David MacBrayne's W. Highland services. War duties under white ensign. Has made frequent appearances on Ardrishaig route since then. Still in service.

LORD OF THE ISLES (1891)—See page 20.

LUCY ASHTON (1888)—See page 16.

MAID OF ARGYLL—Motor, screw, single funnel, lgth. 165 ft. Blt. 1953 A. & J. Inglis, Pointhouse, for CSPC. Originally based at Craigendoran but now on rota of service with other 3 "Maid" class ships.

MAID OF ASHTON—Motor, screw, single funnel, 165 ft. Blt. 1953 Yarrow & Co., for CSPC. Chiefly on Holy Loch run from Gourock until recently. Still in service.

MAID OF BUTE—Motor, screw, single funnel. Blt. 1937 at Fraserburgh and owned by J. Knox, Rothesay, but in 1966 made connections out of that resort for the CSPC. Still in service.

MAID OF CUMBRAE—Motor, screw, single funnel, lgth. 165 ft. Blt. 1953 Ardrossan Dockyard Co., for CSPC. Excursions, railway connections and tendering duties in rotation with other 3 "Maid" class ships.

MAID OF SKELMORLIE (1953)—See page 48.

MADGE WILDFIRE (1886)—See page 14.

MARCHIONESS OF BREADALBANE—Steam, paddle, single funnel, lgth. 200 ft. Blt. 1890 J. Reid & Co., Port Glasgow, for CSPC. Services out of Gourock and Wemyss Bay, long association with Millport run. Minesweeper in war. Sold 1935 for cruise work at Yarmouth and Lowestoft and broken up in Germany 1936.

MARCHIONESS OF BUTE—Steam, paddle, single funnel, lgth. 200 ft. Blt. 1890 J. Reid & Co., Port Glasgow, for CSPC. Services Gourock/ Wemyss Bay railway connections. Sold 1908 for service on the Tay and minesweeping during war years. Broken up 1925.

MARCHIONESS OF GRAHAM—Steam, screw, single funnel, lgth. 220 ft. Blt. 1936 Fairfield, Govan, for CSPC. Intended mainly for Ardrossan/Arran service but during and since war performed various duties. Sold to Greek owners 1958.

MARCHIONESS OF LORNE—Steam, paddle, single funnel, lgth. 200 ft. Blt. 1891 J. & G. Thomson, Clydebank, for CSPC. Normally on Wemyss Bay/ Millport run in season, on Ardrossan/Arran service in winter, excellent sea boat. War service in Mediterranean and returned in poor condition. Lay in Bowling Harbour and broken up Dumbarton 1923.

MARCHIONESS OF LORNE—Steam, paddle, single funnel, lgth. 199 ft. Blt. 1935 Fairfield, Govan, for CSPC's Gourock/Holy Loch run. Seldom deviated from this route and remained on Clyde during war. Spent last year on service (1953) on Wemyss Bay/Millport/Kilchattan Bay run. Broken up Port Glasgow 1955.

MARMION (1906)—See page 32.

MARQUIS OF BUTE—Steam, paddle, single funnel, lgth. 196 ft. Blt. 1868 Barclay Curle, Glasgow, for A. & T. McLean. Service Glasgow to Rothesay. Became one of the bought-in G & SWR fleet in 1891 and usually on Fairlie/Millport run. Sold to Ireland 1904.

MARS—Steam, paddle, single funnel, lgth. 200 ft. Blt. 1902 John Brown, Clydebank, for G & SWR's Princess Pier/Holy Loch route. Played her part in most of the "Sou' West" services. As minesweeper HMS Marsa in 1914/18 war sunk by collision with destroyer at Harwich.

MEG MERRILIES—Steam, paddle, twin funnels, lgth. 210 ft. Blt. 1883 Barclay Curle, Glasgow, for NB railway connections from Craigendoran. After one year returned to builders as deficient in speed. Purchased by Captain Robert Campbell for his Holy Loch service, one funnel removed. Passed with his business in 1889 to CSPC. Sold to Brazil 1902.

MERCURY—Steam, paddle, single funnel, lgth. 220 ft. Blt. 1892 Napier, Shanks & Bell, for G & SWR. Very fast. Service normally Princess Pier to Rothesay and Kyles of Bute. Strenuous war service in which she lost both bow and stern through mines. Returned to Clyde and sailed until 1933 when sold to Barrow for scrapping.

MERCURY—Steam, paddle, single funnel, lgth. 223 ft. Blt. 1934 Fairfield, Govan, for LMS. First Clyde vessel to have rectangular shaped "disguised" paddleboxes On Princes Pier/Kyles of Bute service. Taken for minesweeping duties and mined in Irish Sea, Christmas Day 1940.

MINARD—Steam, screw, single funnel, lgth. 143 ft. Blt. 1926 Scott & Sons, Bowling, for Clyde Cargo Steamers. Cargo and limited passenger service Glasgow to the coast. Transferred to BTC 1949. Broken up 1955.

MINARD CASTLE—Steam, screw, single funnel, lgth. 140 ft. Blt. 1882 J. Fullerton & Co., Paisley, for Lochfyne & Glasgow SP Co. Cargo and limited passenger accommodation Glasgow and coast ports. Later a unit of Clyde Cargo Steamers fleet. Broken up 1928.

MINERVA—Steam, paddle, single funnel, lgth. 200 ft. Blt. 1893 J. & G. Thomson, Clydebank, for G & SWR services from Princes Pier. Sister ship of Glen Rosa. Retained by Admiralty after serving as minesweeper during 1914/18 war. Eventually sold to Turkish owners and broken up 1927.

MOUNTAINEER—Steam, paddle, single funnel, lgth. 180 ft. Blt. 1910 A. & J. Inglis, Pointhouse, for David MacBrayne's W. Highland services. Made rare appearance on Clyde on winter and relief duties on Ardrishaig and Loch Goil routes. Had spell on charter to NB during 1914/18 war. Broken up Port Glasgow 1938.

NEPTUNE—Steam, paddle, single funnel, lgth. 220 ft. Blt. 1892 Napier, Shanks & Bell, Glasgow, for G & SWR, their first vessel built and very speedy. Started on Ardrossan/Arran route but soon sailing from Princes Pier to Ayr and Stranraer among other cruises. Originally a twin sister of Mercury. Sunk by mine when serving with Navy during 1914/18 war.

PALADIN—Steam, screw, single funnel, lgth 140 ft. Blt. 1913 Murdoch and Murray, Port Glasgow, for tendering work for the Anchor Line. Seen occasionally in the role of pleasure cruise vessel carrying charter parties as far as Campbeltown, ran under charter for Williamson Buchanan 1932, sold 1939 to Clyde Shipping Company.

PIONEER—Steam, paddle, single funnel, lgth. 160 ft. Blt. 1905 A. & J. Inglis, Pointhouse, for David MacBrayne's West Loch Tarbert/Islay run. Made rare winter appearance on Clyde service. Requisitioned by Admiralty in 1944 as headquarters ship for submarines at Fairlie, later taken over permanently and as HMS Harbinger moored in Portland Harbour 1946 and fitted out as floating laboratory.

QUEEN ALEXANDRA—Steam, screw, twin funnels, lgth. 270 ft. Blt. 1902 Denny Bros., Dumbarton, for Turbine Steamers Ltd., 21 knots. Service Princes Pier to Campbeltown or Inveraray. After fire aboard at Greenock 1911 sold to CPR for sailings out of Vancouver.

QUEEN ALEXANDRA—Steam, screw, twin funnels, lgth. 270 ft. Blt. 1912 Denny Bros., Dumbarton, for Turbine Steamers to replace vessel of same name, 21 knots. War service as trooper. 1914/18. war. 1935 transferred to David MacBrayne. Received third funnel in course of extensive refit and renamed Saint Columba. Placed on Ardrishaig run. Accommodation vessel at Greenock during 1939/45 war. Scrapped - Port Glasgow 1959.

QUEEN-EMPRESS—Steam, paddle, single funnel, lgth. 210 ft. Blt. 1912 Murdoch and Murray, Port Glasgow, for John Williamson. Broomielaw to the coast. Minesweeper during 1914/18 war and as hospital ship almost lost at Archangel. Later cruising on Clyde took her as far south as Girvan and Campbeltown. After 1939/45 war duties broken up in Holland.

QUEEN MARY II—See page 40.

ROBINA—Steam, screw, single funnel, lgth. 159 ft. Blt. 1914 Ardrossan Drydock Co., for excursion work at Morecambe. Via Bristol, Blackpool and Belfast Lough arrived in Clyde under flag of Coast Lines. Chartered to D. MacBrayne and employed on Lochgoilhead service in 1947, thereafter going to Channel Islands.

REDGAUNTLET—Steam, paddle, single funnel, lgth 215 ft. Blt. 1895 Barclay Curle, Glasgow, for NB Craigendoran coast services, later used as general cruise steamer and almost lost through going ashore on Arran coast 1899. Transferred to Galloway Saloon SPC on Forth 1909, thereafter minesweeping and sold to Oran. Broken up 1934.

SAINT COLUMBA—See Queen Alexandra 1912.

STRATHMORE—Steam, paddle, single funnel, lgth. 200 ft. Blt. 1897 Russel & Co., Port Glasgow, for John Williamson, a sister ship to Kylemore. Service Glasgow to coast but was on Campbeltown run just prior to the arrival of the turbines. 1908 sold to Admiralty and as HMS Harlequin based at Chatham.

TALISMAN—Steam, paddle, single funnel, lgth. 215 ft. Blt. 1896 A. & J. Inglis, Pointhouse, for NB express service between Craigendoran and coast. Admiralty service 1914/18 war. Returned to peace-time duties with navigation bridge moved forward of funnel. Broken up Barrow 1934.

TALISMAN (1935)—See page 44.

TARANSAY—Motor, screw, single funnel, lgth. 110 ft. Blt. 1930 Hall Russell, Aberdeen, for William McCaig. Served in 1948 on Clyde between Glasgow and Campbeltown, cargo and passenger certificate for 12. Laid up thereafter and back at Aberdeen in mid 'fifties.

TEXA—Steam, screw, single funnel, lgth. 100 ft. (lengthened to 118). Blt. 1884 Scott & Son, Bowling, for W. & J. Mutter. Transferred 1889 to D. MacBrayne for service Glasgow to Lochfyneside. Mainly cargo limited passenger. 1917 sold to Isle of Man.

ULSTER LADY—Motor, screw, single funnel, lgth. 112 ft. One of numerous Fairmile launches built in 1940's. Acquired by John Hall, Kirkcaldy, 1948 and running on Tay as *Royal Tay Lady*, 1949 on Belfast Lough as *Ulster Lady*. Came to Clyde 1950 and on service Princes Pier/ Rothesay/Kyles of Bute for one season. Broken up 1954.

VICEROY—Steam, paddle, single funnel, lgth. 194 ft. (lengthened to 208 ft.). Blt. 1875 D. & W. Henderson, Glasgow, for Capt. Alexander Williamson's "Turkish Fleet"'. Service Glasgow to Rothesay. Acquired 1891 by G & SW for railway connections. 1907 sold to North Wales concern.

VIVID—Steam, paddle, single funnel, lgth. 188 ft. (lengthened to 197 ft.). Blt. 1864 Barclay Curle, Glasgow, for Capt. Robert Campbell's Glasgow/ Holy Loch service. Bought 1884 by Capt. Buchanan for Broomielaw/Rothesay trade. Broken up Renfrew 1902.

VULCAN (1897)—See *Kylemore*.

WAVERLEY—Steam, paddle, single funnel, lgth. 235 ft. Blt. 1899 A. & J. Inglis, Pointhouse, for NB. Very fast. Cruising and railway connections. out of Craigendoran. Alterations for war service included extention of promenade deck forward to the bow. This retained after hostilities. Withdrawn from service at end of season 1938 and lay in Bowling Harbour. Taken for Navy duties again and bombed and sunk at Dunkirk 1940.

WAVERLEY—Steam, paddle, twin funnels, lgth. 240 ft. Blt. 1947 A. & J. Inglis, Pointhouse, for LNER Craigendoran to Arrochar service. Joined nationalised fleet following year and as member of CSPC still cruising out of Craigendoran on various runs.

WEE CUMBRAE—Motor, screw, no funnel, lgth. 59 ft. Blt. 1935 Denny Bros., Dumbarton, for CSPC's Largs/Millport service. Examination vessel in Firth of Clyde during war, later peace-time duties out of Gourock. Sold to North Borneo 1953.

WIMAISIA—Motor, screw, single funnel, lgth. 119 ft. Blt. 1936 Harland & Wolff, Belfast and as *Duchess of Abercorn* running for Belfast Harbour Board. Acquired by William McCaig and sailed on Clyde as *Wimaisia* 1948, Glasgow to Campbel-town. Accommodation 230 passengers. Sold at end of season to Liverpool Fire Service and renamed *William Gregson*.

WINDSOR CASTLE—Steam, paddle, single funnel, lgth. 195 ft. Blt. 1875 T. Seath, Rutherglen, for Lochgoil Co. Practically entire career spent on Broomielaw to Lochgoilhead route. Last run made on Queen's Birthday Holiday 1900. Sold to Turkish owners.